Listen Up

10-Minute Family Devotions on the Parables

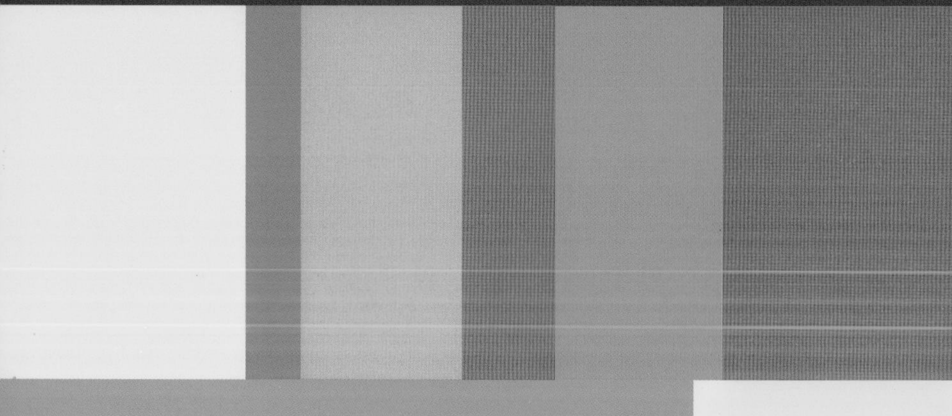

“Parents will love how *Listen Up* scatters the seed of God’s Word into the fertile soil of their children’s hearts. Through clear explanation, hands-on activities, and practical application, Marty Machowski helps families pay attention to the life-changing stories of our Master Teacher. More than a collection of teaching, these pages are nothing less than a map, pointing the way to hidden treasure. *Listen Up*—riches await!

Champ Thornton, Author of *The Radical Book for Kids: Exploring the Roots and Shoots of Faith*

“Biblically faithful. Gospel rich. Theologically insightful. Practical. Creative. Engaging. These are some of the words that came to mind as I read through Marty Machowski’s *Listen Up*! I learned things I didn’t know about the parables, and repeatedly found myself thinking, ‘Parents and their kids are going to benefit so much from this book!’ Marty has obviously done his homework and excels at using the whole Bible to help us understand what Jesus is saying in the parables. Best of all, he consistently points us not only to the words of Jesus, but to Jesus himself as the only Savior of the world.

Bob Kauflin, Director of Sovereign Grace Music

“God gifted Marty Machowski with love for the Bible and profound creativity. In *Listen Up*, he employs these gifts to share Jesus’s parables with the next generation. Children will be engaged by the fun facts and interactive activities. More importantly, they’ll learn to listen to, treasure, and build their lives on the Savior’s words.”

Jared Kennedy, Pastor of Families at Sojourn Community Church Midtown, Louisville, KY; coauthor of *Leadership Mosaic* and *PROOF Pirates VBS*

"If I ever had to return to my child-rearing years, I'd certainly want to take *Listen Up* with me. It is a book of family devotions, written in a lively, vivid style. It presents an accurate account of Jesus's parables and applies them well to the lives of every participant. Machowski includes excellent suggestions for object lessons, group activities, prayer, and 'going deeper,' while keeping the actual meetings under ten minutes! I can't imagine that anyone would follow the book's directions without becoming a better disciple of Jesus."

John M. Frame, Professor Emeritus of Systematic Theology and Philosophy, Reformed Theological Seminary, Orlando, FL

"Marty is a parent's best friend when it comes to figuring out how to creatively and competently do what we really want to do, which is talk with our kids about what matters most—the word of God."

Nancy Guthrie, Author of *Dinner Table Devotions and Discussion Starters*

"Marty Machowski is at it again! With *Listen Up*, Marty has put another tool in parent's hands, helping parents to make wise use of one of Jesus's most common teaching methods: parables. These are some of the most memorable stories in the Bible, and Marty will help you teach them to your kids in unforgettable ways.

C. J. Mahaney, Sovereign Grace Church of Louisville

"Machowski has designed yet another magnificent resource for families. In this new devotional guide he teaches parents and kids how to listen to what God says to us in the parables. The Word of God is alive! We need help to see and understand, and that is what Machowski's devotional guides aim to do. It is wonderfully fitting for this parable genre that Machowski's illustrations shine as brilliant aids for our apprehension of the living Word."

Gloria Furman, Author of *Missional Motherhood* and *Alive in Him*

Listen Up

Listen Up

Ten-Minute Family Devotions on the Parables of Jesus

Marty Machowski

New Growth Press, Greensboro, NC 27404

Cover Design: Faceout Books, faceoutstudio.com
Typesetting: Lisa Parnell, lparnell.com

ISBN 978-1-945270-15-4 (Print)
ISBN 978-1-945270-16-1 (eBook)

Library of Congress Cataloging–in–Publication Data on file

Printed in China

24 23 22 21 20 19 18 17 1 2 3 4 5

Dedication

I dedicate this book to all Christian parents who hold a desire to pass their faith on to their children. May the grace of God strengthen you in your efforts to teach the glorious deeds of the Lord through this book. I pray the Spirit of God opens your eyes wider, to see the wonder of Christ far deeper. Then your children will observe the resulting joy, beaming upon your face and be stirred to follow in your way. Anyone can pass along information; but with the Scriptures we offer our children a far richer heritage. For the Lord you see, has risen; he is alive, and his Word is living and active. While the Bible does serve to inform, it carries with it the greater power to transform and that's what ensures our feeble efforts to disciple our children, empowered by the Spirit, will reap a harvest of righteousness.

Contents

Acknowledgments

Many thanks to my wife Lois who reads through all of my work and the pastoral team at Covenant Fellowship Church for their ongoing encouragement to keep writing. I would also like to thank New Growth Press for their dedication to providing strong biblical resources for churches and families to use and their desire to pass on the gospel to the next generation.

This work would not be possible if it were not for the help of the scholars who have studied the parables before me and committed their knowledge to paper. I would especially like to thank Simon Kistemaker for his book: *The Parables, Understanding the Stories Jesus Told*; Gary Inrig and his book: *The Parables, Understanding What Jesus Meant*; John Macarthur and his book: *Parables, The Mysteries of God's Kingdom Revealed Through the Stories Jesus Told*; Klyne R. Snodgrass for his book, *Stories with Intent, A Comprehensive Guide to the Parables of Jesus*; and finally the great Baptist scholar and pastor Benjamin Keach for his 900-page *Exposition of the Parables and Express Similitudes of Our Lord and Saviour Jesus Christ*. I recommend all of these for further study.

The greatest thanks, however, are reserved for God, without his grace and strength, writing this book would simply not be possible. It is my desire to keep my hands on the plow, not look back, and attribute every step forward to God's sustaining, and empowering grace. To God be the glory.

Introduction

Listen Up is a devotional designed to help families explore the parables of Jesus. A parable is a short story, word picture, or figure of speech. The word *parable* means "thrown beside." Jesus shared parables alongside his sermons for two reasons—to spark the curiosity of those who wanted to learn, while often disguising the truth from the skeptics. After teaching a parable Jesus often said, "He who has ears to hear, let him hear" (Matthew 11:15). In other words, "this is important, so you better listen up."

Later, when Jesus was alone with his disciples, and anyone else who wanted to listen, he explained everything to them (Mark 4:34), opening their eyes and minds to the truth the parables were meant to convey. Today we have many of these explanations preserved for us in the gospels. They form the foundation for our understanding of the parables and how to interpret these stories and word pictures.

Children love stories, and the parables provide a wonderful opportunity to engage their imaginations and help them understand key biblical truths. It is interesting that one of the Bible's most ardent supporters of teaching children predicted Jesus would one day speak in parables. His name was Asaph the Seer. More than one thousand years before Jesus walked the earth, during the reign of King David, Asaph prophesied that Jesus would one day teach with parables. This is what he said:

> *Give ear, O my people, to my teaching;*
> *incline your ears to the words of my mouth!*
> *I will open my mouth in a parable;*
> *I will utter dark sayings from of old,*
> *things that we have heard and known,*

that our fathers have told us.
We will not hide them from their children,
but tell to the coming generation
the glorious deeds of the LORD, *and his might,*
and the wonders that he has done (Psalm 78:1–4).

As we explore the parables, let's make Asaph's passion our own. Asaph loved the Lord and all his glorious deeds. He also loved children and wanted more than anything else to pass on his love of God to the next generation.

Sing the Proverbs with the *Listen Up* companion music CD, available from Sovereign Grace Music at http://sovereigngracemusic.org/music/albums/

For Parents

Each of the thirteen weeks of this study begins with a short overview entitled, "Get Ready." If you start your study on Sunday, you can read through the Get Ready section and then begin the activity found in the following "Get Set" section.

The Get Ready and Get Set sections will provide your family with a preview of the topic of study as well as a corresponding activity. In the Get Ready section, we present an action word of the week. This helps introduce the theme of that week's devotions and provides a single word to help your children apply what they are learning. We'll introduce words like believe, trust, pray, give, and treasure, for example.

There are five lessons for each week of devotions. During the week we will study the verses that set up the context, the parables themselves and any follow up teaching Jesus offered the disciples. Some of the parables are short, while others are quite long. But since parables are stories, even younger children should be able to follow along the lengthier passages. We've included the Bible text (English Standard Version) in the lesson so that you do not need to flip back and forth between your Bible and the devotional. In addition to the narrative parables, we also review many of the similitudes, figures of speech, and illustrations Jesus used in his teaching.

Each Bible passage is followed by a short explanation for you to read to your family. This brief commentary will help you and your children understand the key points from the Bible passage you just read. Each week we add a fun fact to break up the more serious teaching. Some of the topics, like Jesus's teaching on heaven and hell, may be a bit sobering for your children. But we've not included anything your children wouldn't read in a simple review of the gospels. It is recommended to read through the week's devotions yourself prior to introducing them to your family. Consider using them for your personal devotions. Then you will be familiar with the material and more prepared to shepherd your children through the study.

At the end of each lesson we provide you with three questions to ask—and of course, we give you the answers too! There are a few questions where parents are encouraged to share from their lives. Kids love to hear mom and dad talk about when they were young or about a struggle they had but often we keep that history to ourselves. If you review the week prior to your family devotions, you'll be ready for these invitations for you to share from your own life.

We close each lesson with a prayer suggestion. Feel free to lead your family in this time or ask one of your children to do so.

We've also included supplemental sections for parents. Each week begins with a "Look at the Week" to give parents an overview of the lesson. This will help you better understand the context and material. Each lesson ends with a section entitled, Going Deeper, which is also designed to deepen your understanding of the topics covered in the Bible passages. Read through the lessons and use them for your own personal devotions first. Then when you review the devotions with your children you can look for a way to share, in your own words, the information you've learned.

You can also use the introductions and Going Deeper material to challenge older children. If you have grade school children and teens, have your teenage children read these extra study sections and invite them to help you teach their younger brothers and sisters by adding to the discussion things they've learned.

One of the most common questions from parents is, "When should I do devotions with my children?" There is no correct time, but there are three favorites times that many families use. The top choice for families with children of different ages is just after dinner, before dessert. The evening meal is ideal as it already draws families together. Families with children close in age often use bedtime for devotions. If your children are early risers, holding family devotions in the morning can be a great way to start your day. Don't be discouraged if you stop and get derailed—just try again and start from where you left off. You might find that after a week or two, your children will remind you.

Don't feel pressure to perform incredible devotions each session. We don't win our children by entertaining them, the Spirit of God wins our children for Christ as we are faithful to share the good news of Christ with them. So rather than looking to be fantastic, just look to be faithful.

One Final Word about Asaph

Asaph faithfully passed on the glorious deeds of the Lord to his children and trusted God for the results. His children, who learned from his example, did the same. During Asaph's day, four thousand Levites were assigned to play music at the dedication of Solomon's temple and Asaph and his sons were chosen to join them. Over 400 years later, after the temple was destroyed and the foundation rebuilt, the descendants of Asaph, 148 men, were the only singers left, and they were still able to sing and play.

> *And when the builders laid the foundation of the temple of the* Lord*, the priests in their vestments came forward with trumpets,* ***and the Levites, the sons of Asaph, with cymbals, to praise the Lord, according to the directions of David king of Israel****. And they sang responsively, praising and giving thanks to the* Lord*, "For he is good, for this steadfast love endures forever toward Israel." And all the people shouted with a great shout when they praised the* Lord*, because the foundation of the house of the* Lord *was laid* (Ezra 3:10–11 bold emphasis mine).

It is my prayer that Listen Up will help you as a parent tell the next generation the glorious deeds of the Lord. It is my desire that your children will grow up and do the same. It is my hope that your great far off grandchildren, four hundred years from today, will still be serving the Lord and point back to your faithfulness in their lives.

Week 1

Do You Have Ears to Hear?

Let's Look at the Week. . .

The Parable of the Sower appears in Matthew, Mark, and Luke's gospels (Matthew 13, Mark 4, and Luke 8). Each of these gospels retells the parable a bit differently, so it can be helpful to read more than one gospel account to compare them. This week we will read the parable from both Matthew and Luke's gospels. Listen carefully for the differences and see what you can learn by comparing the stories.

The people Jesus taught were familiar with farmers sowing seed in fields. Farmers sowed seed by hand, casting it from a sack hung from a strap around his neck. He would reach in, grab a handful of seed and then broadcast it over the ground. Even the most experienced farmer could not completely control where all the seeds fell.

While the people understood the images in the parable, they would not have understood the meaning behind them. That's why the disciples questioned Jesus and asked him why he taught in parables. Why not tell the people exactly what you want them to learn? You might be surprised to discover that many of the parables were designed to hide the truth, not make it clearer.

Get Ready

The action word of the week is listen.

Listen is a word we use to encourage people to pay careful attention to their surroundings, specifically to things they might otherwise miss. If you hear rain dripping on the windowpane you might say, "Listen, I think it is raining outside. Do you hear the raindrops?"

Listen is also a word we use to encourage a person to pay attention to the instruction they hear. Teachers ask their students to listen carefully to the lessons they teach so that they can learn. Parents, ask their children to listen to their instructions, which means they want them to follow and obey what they say. If your dad says, "Listen, I want you to take out the trash to the street before it gets dark," he doesn't just want you to hear his words, he also wants you to obey his request and take out the trash. So listening is more than hearing. Listening is hearing and doing.

This week we will begin our study of the parables. Our book is called *Listen Up* because it is important to both hear the words that Jesus taught and then apply them to your life by following what they say. A lot of people heard what Jesus taught—they could repeat back to you what they heard. But not everyone was truly listening. So, as we begin our study, make sure you open your ears and listen carefully.

Exploring the Four Soils

(The purpose of this activity is to observe the differences between the four types of soil.)

You can find the four soil types described in the Parable of the Sower in nearly every neighborhood. Weather permitting, after completing today's lesson take your children on a hunt for the four types of soil described in today's parable. Otherwise, simply collect the following supplies and continue with the activity.

Supplies:

- 3 plastic cups
- A handful of rocks or gravel
- A dozen plastic forks
- A handful of soft fertile potting soil
- A piece of modeling dough flattened into a pancake and allowed to dry

Discuss the four types of soil with your children as you experiment with these concepts and materials.

Path—Show your children the dried out dough. Tell them to pretend their index finger is a root popping out of a sprouting seed. Can they get their root into the soil? (No, they cannot.) Why not? (The soil is too hard to allow the root to find a footing.)

Rocky Soil—Fill a cup with gravel. Ask your children to pretend their index finger is a root going down into the rocks. Describe what it feels like to go down into the rocks. (It is difficult and hurts a bit.) What does the parable say is going to happen when the sun comes out? (The plant will shrivel up.)

Weedy Soil—Fill a cup with potting soil and then push several forks down into the soil. Ask your children to try and push their index fingers down into the cup. How easy is it to push your finger down into the soil? (It is difficult because the forks [weeds] are in the way.) What does the parable say happens to the seeds that do sprout in the weedy soil? (The weeds choke them out.) Discuss the likelihood of the weeds stealing the sunlight from the tiny growing plants.

Fertile soil—Fill a cup with fresh potting soil (slightly damp). Have your children push their index finger down into the soil. What does the fertile soil feel like? (It is very soft and it is easy to push your finger down.) If your finger was the root of a sprouting seed, do you think the plant would grow healthy in this soil? (Yes, the fertile soil is free of weeds and rocks and is very soft, making it easy for the young roots to take hold.)

Day One

Listen Up

Read Matthew 13:1–9:

> *That same day Jesus went out of the house and sat beside the sea. And great crowds gathered about him, so that he got into a boat and sat down. And the whole crowd stood on the beach. And he told them many things in parables, saying: "A sower went out to sow. And as he sowed, some seeds fell along the path, and the birds came and devoured them. Other seeds fell on rocky ground, where they did not have much soil, and immediately they sprang up, since they had no depth of soil, but when the sun rose they were scorched. And since they had no root, they withered away. Other seeds fell among thorns, and the thorns grew up and choked them. Other seeds fell on good soil and produced grain, some a hundredfold, some sixty, some thirty. He who has ears, let him hear."*

Think about It

Imagine a young boy going out to play after church on Sunday, still wearing a pair of brand new dress shoes. As he races through the kitchen, his mom catches him by the arm, looks him in the eye, and says, "Don't get your new shoes muddy, stay on the driveway, the yard is a mess." Even though the boy heard his mother's words, he must now decide if he will listen to them. Remember, his mom caught him speeding through the kitchen. He seems rather intent on playing outside with his brother.

Ten minutes later, while playing catch on the driveway, an errant pass lands in the middle of the muddy lawn. Now what will the boy do? He might think, "I'll just tiptoe out on the grass to get the ball. After all, he reasons, *I'm not playing on the grass, just retrieving my ball.* Soon the ball is in the grass again and off he goes after it. By the third time, he forgets to tiptoe and after retrieving about ten balls, notices that his brand new shoes are covered in mud. While he heard his mother's words, he didn't listen (follow) her teaching.

When Jesus finished telling the parable of the sower he said, "He who has ears, let him hear." Well of course everyone he spoke to had ears. They heard his words, but could they put his words into practice? With some parables, the meaning was easy to understand. But this parable was different. It was hard to figure out what Jesus was trying to teach. Why did he tell a story about a farmer casting his seed on different kinds of soil? What the people didn't realize was that this parable carried a hidden message. Jesus used a kind of secret code. If you didn't know what the objects in the parable represented, there was no way of understanding the parable or putting it into practice.

The people of Jesus heard what he said and they even understood that seeds sown among rocks, thorns, or along the path would not do well. They all had experience pulling weeds, and tossing rocks out of their gardens. They knew farmers had to plow up hard ground. But because they didn't know what these things represented, they must have wondered, "Why are you telling this to us Jesus? What is the purpose of your story?"

Imagine if the mom in our story told her son a parable instead of simply telling him not to dirty his shoes. "There once was a baker that dropped a fresh loaf of bread on the dirty floor. If you have ears listen up." If she didn't explain the meaning of the parable, the boy would never understand that she was trying to tell him not to dirty his shoes. The only way for the boy to understand she was talking about shoes, not bread would be for him to ask for an explanation.

When Jesus said, he who has ears, let him hear, he was challenging his audience to discover the meaning of his words. In a sense, Jesus is saying, "there is something very important in what I just said. You better figure out what it is." Jesus's little saying did the trick. The disciples came to him asking, "What does this parable mean?" Later this week we will study the explanation Jesus gave them so that we can understand the hidden message of the parable.

Talk about It

▶ Can you remember a time your mom or dad gave you an instruction but you forgot what they said and didn't follow it? *(Parents, help your children remember the times they didn't brush their teeth when you told them or forgot to put their clothes away, or something similar.)*

▶ Why did Jesus say, "He who has ears, let him hear?" *(Jesus was emphasizing the importance of his teaching and reminding them to listen and understand its meaning.)*

▶ What do you think the Parable of the Sower means? *(Allow your children to guess, but hold off until our third lesson to tell them if they are correct. If they give the correct interpretation, ask them how they knew it. Since this is a popular parable, many children learn about it in Sunday school and have already heard Jesus's explanation.)*

Pray about It

Pray to Jesus and ask for the Holy Spirit's help to understand and follow his teaching.

Going Deeper

The parables force people to either come to Jesus with their questions or ignore him all together. Parables help expose whether or not we want to know Jesus better.

Jesus often spoke to two different audiences at the same time. The first group was comprised of those whom he called—the disciples, or those drawn by the Father. They loved to be around Jesus and listen to his teaching. The other audience included religious rulers who were jealous of Jesus and didn't like him at all.

We want our children to see the difference between these two audiences and encourage them to be listeners and followers of Jesus.

Shortly before he went to the cross Jesus taught the disciples about the Holy Spirit he would soon send. He said, "the Helper, the Holy Spirit, whom the Father will send in my name, he will teach you all things and bring to your remembrance all that I have said to you" (John 14:26).

The Holy Spirit is still in the business of helping us understand the teaching of Jesus and reminding us of what we've learned. Whenever we read the Bible we can pray and ask the Holy Spirit to help us understand much like the disciples asked Jesus to explain his teaching.

Day Two

Listen Up

Read Matthew 13:10–13:

> *Then the disciples came and said to him, "Why do you speak to them in parables?" And he answered them, "To you it has been given to know the secrets of the kingdom of heaven, but to them it has not been given. For to the one who has, more will be given, and he will have an abundance, but from the one who has not, even what he has will be taken away. This is why I speak to them in parables, because seeing they do not see, and hearing they do not hear, nor do they understand."*

Think about It

Some parables are easy to understand. The parable of the Wise and Foolish Builders that we will study next week is like that. But many of the other parables Jesus taught are difficult to discern. Unless you know what the characters and objects represent, you won't understand the true meaning. For example, if I told you the seed in the parable stood for a football, the sower a quarterback, and the weeds represented the opposing football team's linebackers, you would come up with an entirely different interpretation for the parable than the one Jesus gave to his disciples.

The disciples asked Jesus why he taught using parables since the people could not understand the meaning. Why not just teach the people what you want them to learn? Jesus gives a surprising answer. He didn't want them to understand! By disguising truth in parables, Jesus hid it from those who were mocking him and rejecting his teaching. So many of the parables are like a secret code. If you don't have the decoder (know what the parts stand for) many of the parables don't make sense. In order to understand, people needed to seek Jesus for answers. But those who didn't care for Jesus, left confused, thinking he was crazy.

So you see, the parables themselves show us whether or not we want to know Jesus better. Some people say the Bible is confusing and it's too hard to understand. But if you listen carefully to what you read and look for the passages where Jesus explains his teaching, the Bible is fairly easy to understand, and very helpful.

Talk about It

▶ Why did Jesus teach in parables? *(Jesus taught in parables so that people would seek him for understanding. Parables encouraged the practice of asking questions and waiting for answers. We can all have that same type of relationship with Jesus today.)*

▶ If Jesus were here right now, what questions would you have for him? *(Parents, you can use this question to help your children become active listeners. As they listen carefully, they may think of additional questions in need of answers.)*

▶ What information do you need to understand the meaning behind a parable? *(You need to know what the people or things in the parable represent.)*

▶ What are the secrets of the kingdom of heaven that Jesus hid from the religious rulers by teaching in parables? *(The gospel message is the secret of the kingdom. Jesus came as the promised Messiah who would die on the cross to take away the sins of the people of God and restore their relationship to God. The Pharisees and other religious rulers refused to believe he was the Messiah and they sure did not want to give up their power to a new king.)*

Pray about It

Thank God for showing us the secrets of the kingdom in the Bible. We are able to read the parables and understand them through the teachings of Jesus.

Going Deeper

The Pharisees and other religious rulers often came to trap Jesus, not to learn (Mark 12:13 and Luke 20:20). By teaching with parables, the truth of the gospel remained hidden from them. But for those who wanted to learn, Jesus was glad to explain the hidden meaning. The Scriptures tell us Jesus explained everything to his disciples. There is only one Pharisee, Nicodemus, who came back privately to ask Jesus more, his story is found in the third chapter of John.

Given the many prophecies describing the coming Messiah, the Pharisees should have recognized Jesus was the promised one. Jesus was a descendant (long far off grandson) of King David, and just as the prophets foretold was born of a virgin in the Bethlehem the City of David. Others called him the Messiah and believed him to be the one who would deliver Israel, but the Pharisees were jealous and refused to believe. Even worse, they spoke against him. Because of their unbelief, Jesus hid the secret message of the gospel from them by speaking in parables. Yet he was glad to explain the parables to anyone who wanted to listen—anyone who had ears to hear.

Day Three

Listen Up

Read Matthew 13:16–23:

> *But blessed are your eyes, for they see, and your ears, for they hear. For truly, I say to you, many prophets and righteous people longed to see what you see, and did not see it, and to hear what you hear, and did not hear it.*
>
> *"Hear then the parable of the sower: When anyone hears the word of the kingdom and does not understand it, the evil one comes and snatches away what has been sown in his heart. This is what was sown along the path. As for what was sown on rocky ground, this is the one who hears the word and immediately receives it with joy, yet he has no root in himself, but endures for a while, and when tribulation or persecution arises on account of the word,*

immediately he falls away. As for what was sown among thorns, this is the one who hears the word, but the cares of the world and the deceitfulness of riches choke the word, and it proves unfruitful. As for what was sown on good soil, this is the one who hears the word and understands it. He indeed bears fruit and yields, in one case a hundredfold, in another sixty, and in another thirty."

Think about It

In our last devotion, we learned that Jesus spoke in parables to hide the truth of his teaching from the religious leaders who mocked and rejected him. But, he also spoke in parables to encourage others to come to him with their questions and begin a relationship with Jesus. In today's Bible passage we see Jesus give the secret code, which helped explain the meaning of the parable to his closest followers and anyone else who wanted to learn. Matthew, who wrote the gospel we read from today, would have been there with the disciples, listening to Jesus explain the parable's meaning.

Jesus wanted the disciples to realize how important the parables were and how blessed they were to understand their meaning. The great saints of old like King David and the prophets such as Isaiah, and Jeremiah longed to hear the promised Messiah speak these truths, but they all died before Jesus was born. Each of the disciples on the other hand were handpicked by Jesus to know him, follow him, and sit under his teaching. They soon became his friends.

As we read Jesus's explanation of the Parable of the Four Soils, we too are blessed like the disciples, for we get to hear the same truth they heard, the message the kings and prophets of old longed to hear. The kings and prophets of old knew God promised to send a deliverer, but they didn't know who he was. We get to look back at the story and meet Jesus for ourselves. We know he is the promised deliverer and we know the end of the story—Jesus died to take away our sin and rose on the third day to new life. But here is the important question: Will we listen to what we read and follow Jesus?

Will our hearts be like fertile soil for his message? Will we believe in Jesus and give him our whole lives?

Remember, only one of the four soils is good soil—representing the one who hears the message and holds on to it and follows it for life. Every person who reads the parable and its true meaning has a choice to make—that is, which soil will they be? How will they respond to the words of life the prophets longed to hear?

Talk about It

▶ Explain the meaning of the parable of the sower in your own words. *(Parents, review the parable going through each of the four soils and Jesus's explanation. See if your children can remember the meaning.)*

▶ Which soil do you want to describe your life? *(Of course the correct answer is the fertile soil. Help your children think of a few good reasons they should want to be like the fertile soil.)*

▶ None of our lives are free of weeds and rocks. How then can the seed of the gospel grow in such imperfect soil? *(Jesus sent his Holy Spirit to help us much like he helped the disciples while he was on earth. While we do have weeds and rocks, the Holy Spirit helps to pluck the weeds and remove the rocks of sin so that the gospel sprouts and grows in our hearts. It is never too late to turn from our sin (repent) and place our trust in Jesus (believe). God is willing to give anyone who calls upon his name a fresh start and a heart that's soft to hear the gospel.)*

Pray about It

Ask God to send his Spirit to help you trust the teachings of Jesus and to be like fertile soil.

SEED DRILLS

Jesus used a number of farming illustrations, but many of these agricultural techniques have changed in the last 2000 years, particularly in the United States. Few families grow their own food and even the way we farm today is not the same. Take the Parable of the Sower, the way we sow seeds today is very different. Did you ever notice how evenly spaced the rows of crops are planted today? That's because modern day farmers use sowing machines called seed drills to plant their seeds. When you sow seeds by hand, casting them across the soil, the sprouting crops are not even, and some patches of your field may not have any plants at all. A seed drill machine uses a row of equally spaced tubes that press into the soil and drop a seed down into the ground. They only drive the seed drill along the fertile soil, so that no seeds are lost to the thorn bushes at the side of the field. Once the seeds are covered, the birds can't see them to snatch them away and when they sprout, you get nice evenly spaced green rows in your field. Consider doing a quick Internet search for the following subjects: farming methods, seed drill photo, and sowing seeds in Africa.

Going Deeper

When Jesus began his ministry he announced to those he taught, "The time is fulfilled, and the kingdom of God is at hand; repent and believe in the gospel" (Mark 1:15). The instructions to repent and believe form the two basic steps all our children must take to become believers. Neither one by itself is sufficient.

The Pharisees tried to repent of sin in their own strength, but refused to believe. Jesus condemned their lives because he saw the sin in their heart. Jesus said, "If you love me you will listen and obey my teaching" (John 14:15 paraphrased). In the book of James, we learn that "even the demons believe—and shudder" (James 2:19).

Everyone who loves Jesus and believes wants to grow in obedience, even though we continue to make mistakes. That's what repentance is all about. When believers fail, we can always run back to Jesus, confess our sin and look to follow him afresh. What a comfort to know that everyone who comes to Jesus is appointed by God to bear lasting fruit (John 15:16). While Jesus calls us to obey, it is the Holy Spirit, our helper, who changes our hearts, and empowers us to follow Jesus.

Day Four

Listen Up

Read Luke 8:9–15:
(We are taking a look at the same parable story we read earlier in the week in Matthew's gospel.)

> *And when his disciples asked him what this parable meant, he said, "To you it has been given to know the secrets of the kingdom of God, but for others they are in parables, so that 'seeing they may not see, and hearing they may not understand.' Now the parable is this: The seed is the word of God. The ones along the path are those who have heard; then the devil comes and takes away the word from their hearts, so that they may not believe and be saved. And the ones on the rock are those who, when they hear the word,*

receive it with joy. But these have no root; they believe for a while, and in time of testing fall away. And as for what fell among the thorns, they are those who hear, but as they go on their way they are choked by the cares and riches and pleasures of life, and their fruit does not mature. As for that in the good soil, they are those who, hearing the word, hold it fast in an honest and good heart, and bear fruit with patience.

Think about It

Some of the parables are found in more than one gospel. It is helpful to compare the stories side by side to see what more we can learn. Matthew, who heard Jesus teaching first hand, gives us an eyewitness account of Jesus's explanation. Luke on the other hand, was not one of the twelve disciples. He wrote his gospel by interviewing people who heard Jesus teach or perhaps those to whom the disciples told the story. Luke then gathered all the information together and wrote an orderly account (Luke 1:3). As a result of his careful investigation, Luke adds a few extra details about Jesus that Matthew did not include.

For example, Luke clearly tells us that the seed in the parable stands for the Word of God. Matthew tells us the birds represent the evil one, while Luke names the evil one as the devil. For those seeds which fell among the thorns, Luke adds a third reason for their failure. In addition to the cares of this life and riches, Luke also warned that the pleasures of life can prevent God's Word from bearing good fruit in our hearts.

On the other hand, Matthew gives us more detail with regard to those represented by the rocky soil. Luke tells us they "believe for a while, and in time of testing fall away." Matthew describes the time of testing as "tribulation and persecution on account of the word." So you can see how reading both accounts, or even adding a third retelling from Mark's gospel (Mark 4:1–20), can help you more fully understand what Jesus taught.

Talk about It

▶ What does the seed represent in the Parable of the Sower? *(The seed is the Word of God sown into a heart—spoken to a person.)*

▶ What are the four different responses to the Word? *(Parents, simply go through Jesus's explanation from today's Bible passage and remind your children any of the four responses they miss.)*

▶ Which soil are you most like, the hardened path, the rocky soil, the thorny soil, or the fertile soil? *(Parents, see if you children can identify themselves with the groups of people presented in the parable.)*

Pray about It

Ask God to plow and soften the soil of your heart, to kill the thorns, remove the rocks, and make your heart ready to receive the seeds of the gospel. Ask for faith to believe the Word of God and trust in Jesus.

Going Deeper

Matthew wrote as an eyewitness. That's one of the main job descriptions of a disciple. Just before he returned to his Father Jesus told his disciples, "you will receive power when the Holy Spirit has come upon you, and you will be my witnesses in Jerusalem and in all Judea and Samaria, and to the end of the earth" (Acts 1:8).

Luke was not an eyewitness or a disciple. He was a doctor. So rather than provide an eyewitness account in his gospel, he went through a process of compiling an accurate account of Jesus's life. In the introduction to the gospel of Luke, he explains this process:

"Inasmuch as many have undertaken to compile a narrative of the things that have been accomplished among us, just as those who from the beginning were eyewitnesses and ministers of the word have delivered them to us, it seemed good to me also, having followed all things closely for some time past, to write an orderly account for you, most excellent Theophilus, that you may have certainty concerning the things you have been taught" (Luke 1:1–4).

Understanding Luke's compilation of stories from eyewitnesses explains how he is able to include additional details that are not found in the other gospels.

Day Five

Listen Up

Read Luke 8:16–18:

> *"No one after lighting a lamp covers it with a jar or puts it under a bed, but puts it on a stand, so that those who enter may see the light. For nothing is hidden that will not be made manifest, nor is anything secret that will not be known and come to light. Take care then how you hear, for to the one who has, more will be given, and from the one who has not, even what he thinks that he has will be taken away."*

Think about It

The Parable of the Lamp Under a Jar directly follows the Parable of the Sower in Luke's gospel. The parable is a simple one. When you light a lamp, you put it on a stand so that it can shine its light into a dark room. It would be silly to then cover up the light to keep the room dark. No one ever does that. Jesus uses a ridiculous story (covering a lit lamp to hide the light) to get our attention. Once again we need to understand what the lamp represents to understand the parable. Sometimes we can get a clue from another part of the Bible. For example, when we read a similar parable in Matthew Jesus says, "You are the light of the world. A city set on a hill cannot be hidden. Nor do people light a lamp and put it under a basket, but on a stand, and it gives light to all in the house. In the same way, let your light shine before others, so that they may see your good works and give glory to your Father who is in heaven" (Matthew 5:14–16).

The lamp represents a person who believes in Jesus. The light is the gospel truth Jesus taught, which has the power to change people's lives.

Jesus ends the short parable with a warning. One day, all that we've done, both good and bad will be brought out into the open and be made known. God is going to judge what we did with the truth we learned from Jesus. Did we follow Jesus's teaching or go our own way? Did we share the message about Jesus with others?

Once again Jesus warns us to "Listen Up" when he says, "Take care then how you hear." Those who listen and follow what Jesus taught are eager to dig into God's Word and learn more. Those who ignore what they learn are not eager to study God's Word, and what they have learned will be forgotten and lost.

It is important to remember that we all fail to follow Jesus, but those who trust in his sufficient work on the cross are forgiven of their sin. When believers stand before God's judgment throne we stand with Jesus. Jesus will tell his Father, "I died to take away his or her sin." On that day, all believers will be welcomed into heaven to shouts of praise.

Talk about It

▶ What does the light of the lamp represent in this parable? *(The light of the lamp represents the truth of Jesus that we as the lamp can share with the dark world around us.)*

▶ What does light do to the darkness? What happens to the darkness in a room when you turn on the light? *(The darkness goes away; it just disappears. When you shine the light of the truth of the gospel it changes people's lives.)*

▶ What darkness goes away when we shine the light of God's truth into our lives? *(The darkness of sin and evil are sent away by the truth of God's Word. It acts like a light to dispel sin and evil by helping us to know the wonderful truth about Jesus.)*

Pray about It

Ask God to help you listen and obey all that Jesus taught so that your life will be like a lamp on a stand, shining the truth of God's Word for everyone to see.

Going Deeper

The very first person to tell anyone about Jesus was John the Baptist. When John's father, Zechariah, prophesied over his newborn son, he spoke of the light:

> "And you, child, will be called the prophet of the Most High; for you will go before the Lord to prepare his ways, to give knowledge of salvation to his people in the forgiveness of their sins, because of the tender mercy of our God, whereby the sunrise shall visit us from on high to give light to those who sit in darkness and in the shadow of death, to guide our feet into the way of peace." (Luke 1:76–79)

Jesus told his disciples to go into the entire world and share his story and teaching with the people they met (Matthew 28:19–20). In a sense, he was telling them to put his light on display for all to see. When we tell others about Jesus we are shining the light of the gospel too. When Jesus taught a similar parable in Matthew's gospel he explained it saying, "You are the light of the world. A city set on a hill cannot be hidden. Nor do people light a lamp and put it under a basket, but on a stand, and it gives light to all in the house. In the same way, let your light shine before others, so that they may see your good works and give glory to your Father who is in heaven" (Matthew 5:14–16).

Week 2

Building on the Rock

Let's Look at the Week. . .

The Parable of the Wise and Foolish Builders is one of the easiest parables to understand and yet one of the most important. Through this one little story of two builders, Jesus gives us the tools we need to learn and grow from the parables. But the first thing we must do is open our ears and understanding—we need to listen.

The second thing we need is to apply the teaching of the parables to our lives. If we don't allow the parables to affect our behavior, they won't change our lives. We must come to the parables of Jesus asking the Holy Spirit to convict us of sin and help us to see areas in which we can grow. Then, when the Spirit of God reveals an area that we should change in our lives, we can pray and ask God to help us have ears to hear and grace to change. While we can't change on our own, the Holy Spirit helps us.

The apostle Paul taught that we work together with God as we grow. We obey, but it is God who helps us obey. Paul wrote, "Therefore, my beloved, as you have always obeyed, so now, not only as in my presence but much more in my absence, work out your own salvation with fear and trembling, for it is God who works in you, both to will and to work for his good pleasure" (Philippians 2:12–13). The only way to grow is by listening to what Jesus teaches and then following what he says. That's just what the Parable of the Wise and Foolish Builders is all about. What Paul adds is the part God plays behind the scenes to help us.

Jesus taught the Parable of the Wise and Foolish Builders at the very end of his Sermon on the Mount. This week we will look at several parts of that sermon, but first we will study the parable Jesus shared at the end of his teaching.

Get Ready

The action word of the week is build.

The word *build* means to construct, as in stacking blocks to make a tower. God loves to build things. He built the tall mountains and great valleys when he created the earth. He built the heavens with more stars in the sky than we can count. God also gave us the desire and ability to create things on our own. If you dump a bin of wooden blocks on the floor, you don't have to encourage children to create. Within minutes the floor will be covered with castles and towers.

But if you wait long enough you'll see trouble on the horizon. If a child tries to build a tower too tall, it might come crashing down. One child may knock down another's tower or try to take all the best blocks for themselves. Sins like selfishness and anger spoil the work. So while it is wonderful to build things, it is also important that we pay attention to how we are building.

This week we will study the Parable of the Wise and Foolish Builder. Jesus taught the parable to help us build wisely. Keep your ears open and listen to this week's lesson so you too can become a wise builder.

Sand and Stone

(The purpose of this activity is to identify the differences between rock and sand. In doing so, your children will better understand the illustration of the parable.)

Supplies:

- A bucket of sand
- A fist-sized rock

Hold the rock in your hand and pass it around to your family. Have each person hold the rock and share one word to describe it. Here are a few words to describe the rock: hard, heavy, solid, strong, and firm.

Now take a fist full of sand from the bucket and try to pass it around from person to person. (You might want to do this over the bucket to catch the sand that falls from your hand.) Ask each person share one word to describe the sand. Here are a few words to describe the sand: shifting, gritty, cool, loose, moving, and difficult to grasp.

Finally, discuss how the rock and the sand are very different from one another.

Day One

Listen Up

Read Matthew 7:24–27:

"Everyone then who hears these words of mine and does them will be like a wise man who built his house on the rock. And the rain fell, and the floods came, and the winds blew and beat on that house, but it did not fall, because it had been founded on the rock. And everyone who hears these words of mine and does not do them will be like a foolish man who built his house on the sand. And the rain fell, and the floods came, and the winds blew and beat against that house, and it fell, and great was the fall of it."

Think about It

When Jesus says, "Everyone who hears these words of mine," we should automatically question, "What words?" The answer is very simple—the words Jesus just finished teaching to the crowd. Jesus wanted the crowd to be sure to listen to what he was saying and apply his teaching to their lives. He wanted his words to change the way they lived. He didn't just want them to hear his words, he wanted the crowd to follow them.

Jesus used the example of building a house on the sand to warn the people not to ignore his words. If you ever built a sand castle on the beach, you know how easily it crumbles when the waves strike against it. If you build a house on the sand, instead of on the rock, the waves will come and wash away the sand and the house will fall. But those who listen and obey are like a wise man who builds his house on solid rock—it is easy to see he is making the better choice.

This week we are going to read through some of what Jesus taught to the people on that mountain. But, since we read the parable first, we have a big advantage over that crowd. As we hear Jesus's words, let's be sure to listen carefully and obey (follow) Jesus. If we do, we will be like the man who built his house on the rock. Every time we read the Bible, we have the same choice to make. We can either build on the rock (trusting Jesus by following his teaching) or forget what we read and end up like the man who built his house upon the sand.

Talk about It

▶ Who are the two men that Jesus describes in the parable? *(The two men are the wise man who built his house on the rock and the foolish man who built his house on the sand.)*

▶ Why is it better to build your house on the rock? *(A foundation of rock will not collapse or be washed away in a storm.)*

▶ Jesus is actually talking about people's lives, not giving construction advice for house building. What kinds of storms come into our lives that can wash away a weak foundation—a house built upon sand? *(Parents, help your kids here. They don't have many life experiences to draw from. Here are a couple examples of life's storms: an injury or sickness prevents you from doing something you love, testing your trust in God, or someone performs better than you in an activity, tempting you to become jealous or even unkind toward that person.)*

Pray about It

Ask God to help you live a life of faith and repentance, building your house on the rock—listening and obeying the Bible's teaching through the strength he provides.

Going Deeper

The first question we should ask when reading any passage from the Bible is what was going on back in the day when it was first taught? A quick read of today's passage tells us Jesus was teaching. The next obvious question is who is he teaching? If we search the earlier verses we learn that Jesus is preaching a sermon to a large crowd.

Figuring out all that background is called the context. Once we know the context (the what was going on in real life back in the day), we can better understand why Jesus taught a particular parable. In looking at our Bible passage, we see that the Parable of the Wise and Foolish Builder came at the end of a long sermon that Jesus preached on top of a mountain to a large crowd. This crowd seems interested in learning from Jesus—it is not the jealous, critical, Pharisees that Jesus is speaking to. Here we find people who want to learn. The real question is, will they apply what they are hearing to their lives?

Day Two

Listen Up

Read Matthew 5:1–16:

> *Seeing the crowds, he went up on the mountain, and when he sat down, his disciples came to him.*
>
> *And he opened his mouth and taught them, saying:*
>
> *"Blessed are the poor in spirit, for theirs is the kingdom of heaven.*
>
> *"Blessed are those who mourn, for they shall be comforted.*
>
> *"Blessed are the meek, for they shall inherit the earth.*
>
> *"Blessed are those who hunger and thirst for righteousness, for they shall be satisfied.*
>
> *"Blessed are the merciful, for they shall receive mercy.*
>
> *"Blessed are the pure in heart, for they shall see God.*
>
> *"Blessed are the peacemakers, for they shall be called sons of God.*
>
> *"Blessed are those who are persecuted for righteousness' sake, for theirs is the kingdom of heaven.*
>
> *"Blessed are you when others revile you and persecute you and utter all kinds of evil against you falsely on my account. Rejoice and be glad, for your reward is great in heaven, for so they persecuted the prophets who were before you.*
>
> *"You are the salt of the earth, but if salt has lost its taste, how shall its saltiness be restored? It is no longer good for anything except to be thrown out and trampled under people's feet.*
>
> *"You are the light of the world. A city set on a hill cannot be hidden."*
>
> *"Nor do people light a lamp and put it under a basket, but on a stand, and it gives light to all in the house. In the same way, let your light shine before others, so that they may see your good works and give glory to your Father who is in heaven."*

Think about It

Do you remember what we learned from the parable yesterday? Be sure to keep that lesson in mind as we study today. If we want to be like the man who built his house upon the rock, we can't just read through the Bible. We need to live the Bible by putting it into action. If you are peeling an apple and your mom tells you to be careful, just hearing the words won't keep you from cutting yourself. You actually need to "be careful" to benefit from her warning. But it is also important to remember that we simply can't obey in our own strength. We need the Spirit of God to equip us for this task.

Most people want to look good on the outside—but Jesus cares about what our hearts are like on the inside. Hungering for righteousness means you do more than follow the rules when people are watching. If you really want to live a right life before God—you obey to honor God, even when other people are not watching. Jesus knew the people couldn't do that on their own. He didn't come to give us a list of rules and say, "OK now you need to do it in your own strength." Jesus came to live a perfect life for us and die on the cross in our place. He calls all of us to place our trust in him, not our own strength. When we place our trust in Jesus he gives us his Holy Spirit as our helper to obey him on the outside because we love him on the inside—in our hearts.

When we live like Jesus and follow his Word, his light shines into the darkness of our sinful world. Just like salt makes food taste better, those who place their trust in Jesus bring hope and joy into the world. Think about how much better your food tastes with flavor and seasoning. Jesus can make a similar impact on the world through us.

Jesus didn't just teach these blessings, he lived them out perfectly. Jesus is challenging us to live like he lived (with the Holy Spirit's help) so that we might be like lights shining into the darkness.

Our Bible passage talks about salt losing its saltiness. But how is that possible? Today we have pure white, refined salt, that can't lose its saltiness. But the salt mined from the ground in Jesus's day was very different. The salt was not pure. It was mixed with other minerals, so that if it rained upon a pile of salt, the salt part could wash out, leaving the other minerals behind. It might look like you still have a pile of salt, but with only the other minerals left, the salt pile, which lost its saltiness, was worthless, good for nothing.

Talk about It

▶ Go through Jesus's teaching and count how many different kinds of people he called blessed? *(Parents, just have your kids go through the passage and count the number of times Jesus said "blessed." There are nine total.)*

▶ Is it possible to obey all the qualities Jesus lists to make you blessed? *(None of us can obey Jesus perfectly. We all fail to follow Jesus. That's why Jesus needed to die upon the cross for our sin and live the perfect life we could not live.)*

▶ Who did Jesus send to help us? *(When Jesus went back to be with his Father he sent us the Holy Spirit to show us our sin, open our eyes to believe, and help us to follow Jesus and obey.)*

▶ Read through the list of the beatitudes and use them to encourage one another. Parents, which quality in the list best describes each of your children? Kids, which quality best describes your parents? *(Parents, go first and encourage your children through this list and thereby teach them how to encourage one another through Scripture.)*

Pray about It

Ask God for faith to follow Jesus and live out the Beatitudes.

Going Deeper

In today's Bible passage, Jesus gives us a long list of blessings scholars call the Beatitudes. When we read a list with a lot of repetition, we can be tempted to read it quickly or even skip over some of what we read and miss the importance of each word. Jesus's teaching on the Beatitudes is like that. Think about it—you don't find many coaches, teachers, or bosses teaching these qualities to their players, students, or workers. When was the last time anyone encouraged you to be pure in heart, meek, or to hunger for righteousness?

It was the same in Jesus's day. His teachings were very different from the other religious leaders. That's why he drew such large crowds and that's what made the scribes and Pharisees jealous.

Day Three

Listen Up

Read Matthew 5:17–26:

> *"Do not think that I have come to abolish the Law or the Prophets; I have not come to abolish them but to fulfill them. For truly, I say to you, until heaven and earth pass away, not an iota, not a dot, will pass from the Law until all is accomplished. Therefore, whoever relaxes one of the least of these commandments and teaches others to do the same will be called least in the kingdom of heaven, but whoever does them and teaches them will be called great in the kingdom of heaven. For I tell you, unless your righteousness exceeds that of the scribes and Pharisees, you will never enter the kingdom of heaven.*

"You have heard that it was said to those of old, 'You shall not murder; and whoever murders will be liable to judgment.' But I say to you that everyone who is angry with his brother will be liable to judgment; whoever insults his brother will be liable to the council; and whoever says, 'You fool!' will be liable to the hell of fire. So if you are offering your gift at the altar and there remember that your brother has something against you, leave your gift there before the altar and go. First be reconciled to your brother, and then come and offer your gift. Come to terms quickly with your accuser while you are going with him to court, lest your accuser hand you over to the judge, and the judge to the guard, and you be put in prison. Truly, I say to you, you will never get out until you have paid the last penny.

Think about It

The religious rulers thought they were righteous and good because they never committed serious sins, like murder. They had no idea that getting angry with someone in your heart was a form of that same sin. Without Jesus's teaching to show that anger is the sin of murder, the Scribes and Pharisees would not see any need to trust in Jesus. By teaching them that anger in our heart is also a sin against God, the religious rulers could not claim they were keeping the Law. That upset them even more.

People today know that the sin of murder is wrong. And just like the religious leaders in Jesus day, we make the mistake of thinking we are pretty good because we have never done anything terrible like kill someone. But if you ask the question, "Have you ever been angry and felt like hurting someone?" Everyone would have to answer yes because we have all been sinfully angry inside. The truth is, we all are sinners who need Jesus. We may not have killed anyone, but we've all held anger in our heart against another.

Talk about It

▶ Why is holding anger against a person a sin? *(First, holding anger against a person is a sin because the Bible tells us so. Anger usually involves hurting someone, either with our words like calling them names or with our actions like hitting them. Even if we call them names quietly to ourselves or think bad things about them in our hearts, these are still sinful.)*

▶ Can you remember a time when you got angry with someone? *(Parents, help your children by reminding them of a time when they were angry.)*

▶ Why did Jesus want to show the crowd that they were all sinners? *(Jesus came to die on the cross for their sin. If they thought they were good enough to go to heaven without Jesus, they would not see their need to follow him.)*

Pray about It

Ask God to help you see when you are sinning in your heart so that you will see your need for Jesus.

Going Deeper

For thousands of years, the teachers of Israel taught the law of Moses to the people. The Sermon on the Mount sounded quite a bit different than the law of Moses. Jesus could tell that some of the people thought he wanted to get rid of the Law, especially the other religious rulers and teachers. But Jesus didn't come to throw the Law away. Jesus explained to them that he came to obey and fulfill the Law completely—something no one else could do.

The Scribes and Pharisees believed you could obey the Law sufficiently and taught the people that if a person tried hard enough, they could obey God's commands. The Pharisees made sure that when people were looking, they were doing all the right things. Jesus wanted to help the religious rulers and the people of Israel see that the law of Moses wasn't just about obeying on the outside. Jesus knew that the law of Moses also required we obey on the inside—in our hearts, where we think and feel. That's why Jesus taught that the sin of anger was a form of the sin of murder. Jesus taught that if we hold anger against someone in our heart, we've broken God's Law and committed murder in our hearts.

Day Four

Listen Up

Read Matthew 7:1–12:

> *"Judge not, that you be not judged. For with the judgment you pronounce you will be judged, and with the measure you use it will be measured to you. Why do you see the speck that is in your brother's eye, but do not notice the log that is in your own eye? Or how can you say to your brother, 'Let me take the speck out of your eye,' when there is the log in your own eye? You hypocrite, first take the log out of your own eye, and then you will see clearly to take the speck out of your brother's eye.*
>
> *"Do not give dogs what is holy, and do not throw your pearls before pigs, lest they trample them underfoot and turn to attack you.*
>
> *"Ask, and it will be given to you; seek, and you will find; knock, and it will be opened to you. For everyone who asks receives, and the one who seeks finds, and to the one who knocks it will be opened. Or which one of you, if his son asks him for bread, will give him a stone? Or if he asks for a fish, will give him a serpent? If you then, who are evil, know how to give good gifts to your children, how much more will your Father who is in heaven give good things to those who ask him!*
>
> *"So whatever you wish that others would do to you, do also to them, for this is the Law and the Prophets."*

Think about It

In addition to parables, Jesus also used illustrations. Illustrations are word pictures added to a teaching to help people remember and better understand. The log and the speck is a great example of how a word picture can help us to understand an important point. Imagine how memorable it would be to see Jesus acting out the illustration of the log and speck. The crowd laughs as Jesus pretends to be the person with a log sticking out of his eye, trying to remove a speck from his brother's eye.

Illustrations like this help us to remember important truths. That's why Jesus used them in his teaching. He knew that long after the crowd forgot his teaching on judging others, they would remember the picture the log and speck. (Take time for a quick skit. Have one of your kids pretend to walk around with a log in their eye, trying to remove your speck. Or, for a fun project, cut a couple of holes in the end of a paper towel roll and use a few rubber bands and a piece of yarn to create a band to hold the paper roll on their forehead near their eye to represent the log.) Every time they get close enough to remove a speck they whack the log against the other person.)

Talk about It

▶ What word pictures does Jesus use in today's Bible passage? *(Jesus used the picture of a log and speck, pearls and pigs, dogs, knocking on a door, and a father giving gifts to his children.)*

▶ How do word pictures help us understand what Jesus is teaching? *(Word pictures and illustrations connect Bible truths to everyday life. We can apply what we know about life to help us see the meaning in what Jesus is teaching. People still use these word pictures today, like don't cast your pearls before swine, even though they have no idea that it comes from Jesus's words in Matthew 7.)*

▶ How does knowing God is a loving Father who gives good gifts to his children help you want to pray and ask him for help? *(Parents, draw out your children here and help them to see that God is ready to help them live godly lives. Notice that the children in the word picture are asking for what they need—food and not foolish things that would not be good for them.)*

Pray about It

Take time to learn from today's passage by knocking on God's door—that is praying to him for the things you need. (Parents, help your children come up with something each one can pray.)

Going Deeper

We are good at telling others what they are doing wrong but not so good at seeing our own sin. The truth is that our sin is usually far worse. Too often we look to point out a speck in someone's eye (a small sin) when we have a big log (a big sin) sticking out of our own. The lesson of this word picture teaches us that we should examine ourselves before correcting others. Did you ever notice that when you get into an argument and get angry you like to blame it on the other person? We usually are not so quick to admit what we did to contribute to the conflict but we are quick to point out the other person's faults. Jesus is saying we should look at our own heart first.

Jesus also used several other word pictures in this passage of Scripture. He spoke of a father giving food to a son to help us to understand God's willingness to hear our prayers and help us. The picture of throwing something holy to dogs, or casting pearls to pigs are two other exaggerated illustrations. No one would ever throw pearls to a pig or feed his dog the holy meat from a sacrifice at the temple. Both illustrations are designed to teach that we should not waste our time trying to teach the Word of God to a mocker who will only make fun of it. That's one of the reasons Jesus started teaching truth in parables that were difficult to understand. He wasn't going to teach to those who were going to mock him. Jesus always explained the truth to anyone seeking understanding.

Day Five

Listen Up

Read Matthew 7:13–23:

> *"Enter by the narrow gate. For the gate is wide and the way is easy that leads to destruction, and those who enter by it are many. For the gate is narrow and the way is hard that leads to life, and those who find it are few.*
>
> *"Beware of false prophets, who come to you in sheep's clothing but inwardly are ravenous wolves. You will recognize them by their fruits. Are grapes gathered from*

thornbushes, or figs from thistles? So, every healthy tree bears good fruit, but the diseased tree bears bad fruit. A healthy tree cannot bear bad fruit, nor can a diseased tree bear good fruit. Every tree that does not bear good fruit is cut down and thrown into the fire. Thus you will recognize them by their fruits.

"Not everyone who says to me, 'Lord, Lord,' will enter the kingdom of heaven, but the one who does the will of my Father who is in heaven. On that day many will say to me, 'Lord, Lord, did we not prophesy in your name, and cast out demons in your name, and do many mighty works in your name?' And then will I declare to them, 'I never knew you; depart from me, you workers of lawlessness.'

Think about It

Right before Jesus told the Parable of the Wise and Foolish Builders, he gave a list of warnings using three word pictures. The first describes two paths people follow in life. The path going to heaven is narrow and only a few find it. The path to destruction is broad, and sadly, many people are following it. This path leads to judgment in hell.

The second picture of fruit teaches us that you can tell the condition of a person's heart by observing the fruit they produce in their life. Later in the Bible, Paul tells us the fruit of the Spirit is love, joy, peace, patience, kindness, goodness, faithfulness, gentleness, and self-control (Galatians 5:22–23). When you see this fruit in a person's life you know the Holy Spirit is at work in their heart.

The final word picture presents a serious warning. On the last day, people will call Jesus "Lord." But not everyone who calls Jesus Lord will go to heaven. Jesus knew that it was easy to utter words, but much harder to follow him with our lives.

Talk about It

▸ Think about Jesus's warnings from this passage of the Bible. When you consider these words, what do you need to do to be the wise person who builds his house upon the rock? *(Parents, draw out your children. Consider re-reading today's passage and adding the parable, verses 24–27. Remember the wise person listens to the teaching and obeys it.)*

▸ In light of Jesus's warnings, and knowing we can't just try to do our best, but we need to be perfect, how do we get on the narrow path? *(Parents, this is a wonderful opportunity to share the gospel message with your children again. Explain that Jesus lived a perfect life. He never sinned, even once. Then Jesus died on the cross where God poured out the punishment for the sin of all God's children. Jesus died for our sin and then on the third day rose in victory from the grave. Everyone who recognizes they are a sinner and places their trust in what Jesus did on the cross will be saved. So, the answer is that we need to trust in Jesus to get on the narrow path.)*

▸ What are wolves in sheep's clothing and why do we need to beware of them? *(Wolves in sheep's clothing are people who pretend to love God on the outside, but inside they have not trusted Jesus. We need to be careful because they could lead us down the wrong path.)*

Pray about It

Take time to pray that each person in your family will build their house on the rock, meaning that they will put their trust in Jesus and live for him.

Going Deeper

Jesus spoke to a crowd that thought they could live a righteous (good) life on their own by following the Law. (That's what the religious rulers had been teaching them.) You see, they thought as long as you do the best you can, God will look down and judge your efforts and let you into heaven. But God's standard is perfection. Even one sin separates us from our God, who is holy and perfect in every way. There is also the problem of our sinful nature. Even before we were born, we inherited original sin.

When Adam and Eve sinned against God by eating the forbidden fruit, they passed their sin onto all their children—that means us too, since we are all far off grandchildren of Adam and Eve. All our hearts are sick with sin from birth—we are the diseased trees who bear bad fruit. We need God's Spirit to change us. The good news is that God promises that everyone who places their trust in Jesus and his death for our sin will be forgiven (1 John 1:9), made alive (Ephesians 2:5), and have our hearts changed from hearts of stone to hearts of flesh (Ezekiel 36:26). Trying to do our best doesn't take away our sinful nature—only Jesus can do that.

Week 3

A Treasure, a Pearl, and a Mustard Seed

Let's Look at the Week. . .

Our first week we studied the Parable of the Sower, which is the first of seven parables recorded in Matthew 13. This week we will look at the other six parables. We don't know for sure if Jesus taught all seven parables, one after another in one sermon, or if Matthew pulled them all together because of their similar theme.

We will also look back at the Old Testament. Jesus quoted Asaph from Psalm 78:2 in verse 35. Matthew commented that Jesus taught in parables, revealing the secret message that has been hidden since the beginning of the world. The secret message of course, is the gospel—that Jesus is the Savior who came to defeat sin, death, and to take our punishment and the curse of the fall of Adam and Eve.

After Adam and Eve sinned, eating the forbidden fruit, God promised them that one day a son born to them would crush the head of Satan and thus end the curse which began with their temptation. Though Adam and Eve died without seeing that promised son, their descendants never gave up believing that promised son would come. The prophets longed for that day to come and did their best to try and figure out who this secret son would be (1 Peter 1:12). This week, as we study Matthew's parable chapter, we will learn all about God's kingdom and how from this one man Jesus, God planned to reverse the curse and expand his rule and reign as King over all the earth.

Get Ready

The action word of the week is treasure.

When we think of the word *treasure*, we usually think of something of great worth like gold, diamonds, or pearls. Maybe you think of pirate's treasure; a chest filled with gold coins, buried in the sand on some remote island.

Treasure can be a thing, like gold, diamonds, or pearls, but it can also be something that you do. Treasure is also an action word. For example, a sailor might treasure a picture of his wife, when he is out to sea on a long journey. Even though the picture is not worth any money, the sailor treasures the photo and would never sell it.

Everyone has things they treasure. It could be your favorite stuffed animal that you would never give away, or a picture of your family, your first baseball glove, or you brand new baby sister. We treasure what we love.

This week we will learn that the Bible teaches us to treasure God above all things, even the people we love, like our parents. The Bible doesn't just command us to treasure God, it teaches us the amazing things God has done for us and shows us his great love. Let's listen up and learn all that we can about God and why he is our greatest treasure.

(The purpose of this activity is to consider the common components included in the parables.)

Supplies: (Try to find as many of these items as you can.)

- A plain white plate or platter (this can be disposable)
- A mustard seed (whole mustard seeds can be found in the spice section of your grocery store)
- A slice of bread
- Grain (this can be wheat berries or rice kernels)
- A pearl (any pearl jewelry will do)
- A gold ring (a wedding band or engagement ring is fine)

Place all the items you could find on a plate, spread them out. Gather your children and see how many of the items they can identify. Use the following names:

- Mustard Seed
- Leaven (Explain why bread has bubbles—because yeast or leaven creates bubbles that make it rise.)
- Harvest (Explain that farmers gather the grain at harvest time for food.)
- Pearl (Explain that pearls are grown in oysters and are very valuable.)
- Treasure (Explain that your ring is a treasure because of its great worth.)

Once they finish guessing and you explain the names, tell them that

(continued)

all the items on the plate have something in common. Ask them if they know what they all have in common and give them the following clues:

They are all found in the Bible.

Jesus used them all to teach us about the __________________.

Even with these clues it is likely your children won't be able to give you the answer, the kingdom of heaven. So once you've exhausted their guesses, tell them the answer and explain that the kingdom of heaven is God's rule and reign over the earth.

Jesus used all these items in parables to teach us what the kingdom of heaven is like. While Jesus came to earth as a man, he was also a heavenly King, the Son of God. He came down to earth to win the battle against sin, death, and Satan, and spread his rule of righteousness (goodness) and truth to the whole world. This week we are going to read and talk about the Parables of the Kingdom of Heaven.

Day One

Listen Up

Read Matthew 13:24–30:

> *He put another parable before them, saying, "The kingdom of heaven may be compared to a man who sowed good seed in his field, but while his men were sleeping, his enemy came and sowed weeds among the wheat and went away. So when the plants came up and bore grain, then the weeds appeared also. And the servants of the master of the house came and said to him, 'Master, did you not sow good seed in your field? How then does it have weeds?' He said to them, 'An enemy has done this.' So the servants said to him, 'Then do you want us to go and gather them?' But he said, 'No, lest in gathering the weeds you root up*

the wheat along with them. Let both grow together until the harvest, and at harvest time I will tell the reapers, Gather the weeds first and bind them in bundles to be burned, but gather the wheat into my barn.'"

Think about It

Remember the Parable of the Sower, where the farmer cast seed onto four kinds of soil? The seed in that parable represented the Word of God and the gospel message of salvation. It would be logical to think in reading today's parable that the seed described here also represents that same message, but it doesn't. The seed in this parable represents people. The good seed are God's children born into the world. The seed sown by the enemy represent unbelievers who are not a part of God's family. Unbelievers and believers grow up together just like the good grain grows up mixed with the weeds, living in the same world until the day Jesus returns to judge the world.

Now you might be wondering, "How are you supposed to figure out what the parables mean, if the meaning of the individual parts changes from parable to parable?" Remember, many of the parables were designed to hide important truths from those who didn't care to listen and draw in people who treasured Jesus's teaching and wanted to know more about him. Fortunately for us, Jesus explained today's parable, and gives its interpretation later in the chapter. But, before looking ahead for the meaning in verses 36 to 43, return to the parable (Matthew 13:24–30) and try to discern what you think the following parts of the parable represent (Master, Enemy, Fire and Barn). Then continue on and read verses 36–43 to see if you guessed correctly.

Then he left the crowds and went into the house. And his disciples came to him, saying, "Explain to us the parable of the weeds of the field." He answered, "The one who sows the good seed is the Son of Man. The field is the world, and the good seed is the sons of the kingdom. The weeds are the sons of the evil one, and the enemy who sowed them is the devil. The harvest is the end of the age, and the reapers are angels. Just as the weeds are gathered and burned with fire, so will it be at the end of the age. The Son of Man will send his angels, and they will gather out of his kingdom all causes of sin and all law-breakers, and throw them into the fiery furnace. In that place there will be weeping and gnashing of teeth. Then the righteous will shine like the sun in the kingdom of their Father. He who has ears, let him hear. (Matthew 13:36–43)

Talk about It

▶ Who does Jesus describe as those who will live in heaven—those who will "shine like the sun in the kingdom"? *(The sons and daughters of God, or the good seed sown by Jesus, will live in heaven.)*
▶ What does Jesus mean when he says, "He who has ears, let him hear?" *(When Jesus says, "he who has ears, let him hear," he is saying, "Listen up" and make sure you remember my words and teaching—allow them to change your life.)*
▶ What is the most important lesson we should learn from this parable? *(We should want to make sure we are gathered in with the wheat—the children of God. The only way to ensure that is to turn away from your sin and place your trust in Jesus. If we treasure Jesus more than anything, and turn away from our sin, we can be sure we will be gathered in as the wheat when harvest time comes.)*

Pray about It

Ask God to help you to put your faith and trust in Jesus—the only one who can forgive your sins and make you a Son or Daughter of the King.

Going Deeper

"Listen Up" is the main call of the Parables. Like with the Parable of the Sower, we see the same familiar charge, "he who has ears, let him hear;" in other words, "Listen up" and let the parable affect your life! The most important thing to take away from this parable is to make sure you are a stalk of wheat (a believer in Jesus). The only way to be sure you will be counted with the wheat at the end of the age is to place your trust in Jesus and live for him.

We can't earn our way to God by our works but all Christians show their faith through their good works. Consider what Paul taught to the Ephesians: "For by grace you have been saved through faith. And this is not your own doing; it is the gift of God, not a result of works, so that no one may boast. For we are his workmanship, created in Christ Jesus for good works, which God prepared beforehand, that we should walk in them" (Ephesians 2:8–10).

Paul is clear. We are saved by faith—not works. But also notice that all believers were created for good works that God has prepared for us to walk in. That's why James taught that faith without good works is dead (James 2:17).

Day Two

Listen Up

Read Matthew 13:31–33:

> *He put another parable before them, saying, "The kingdom of heaven is like a grain of mustard seed that a man took and sowed in his field. It is the smallest of all seeds, but when it has grown it is larger than all the garden plants and becomes a tree, so that the birds of the air come and make nests in its branches." He told them another parable. "The kingdom of heaven is like leaven that a woman took and hid in three measures of flour, till it was all leavened."*

Think about It

The parables of Matthew 13 come in pairs. The Parable of the Wheat and the Weeds we talked about yesterday is very similar to one we'll study later in the week called, the Parable of the Fishnet. Two other parables in this chapter, the Parable of the Treasure in a Field and Pearl of Great Price, also go together.

Today's Bible passage contains another pair of parables—the Parable of the Mustard Seed and the Parable of the Leaven. Both parables teach the same lesson. Each one presents a picture of something small growing into something much larger. The mustard seed grows into a great tree and the leaven, or yeast, grows through the whole batch of dough. If you've ever baked bread from scratch, you'll know that yeast causes the dough to expand and double in size. If you look at a slice of bread you'll see the air bubbles, created by the growing yeast, fill every part of the loaf.

Once again, in order to understand the parables, we must determine what or who the items in the parable represent. So, let's begin with the Parable of the Mustard Seed. Who is the sower? What is the mustard seed and what or who are the birds that make nests in its branches?

Fortunately, Jesus gives us a big clue—the parable is meant to teach us about the kingdom of heaven. We also see that the parable presents a story of amazing growth. The tiniest of seeds become a large tree. The mustard that's grown in the west is more like a garden plant, but there is a variety of mustard in Palestine (the place where Jesus lived) that grows into a large tree. A mustard tree in Jesus's day could be taller than a horse and rider. So, the kingdom of heaven is going to start out small and then grow and grow.

The kingdom of heaven is not a building but a family. That family began with God choosing Abraham, from all the peoples in the earth. The Bible tells us that Abraham believed God's promise that one day his offspring would fill the whole earth. From that that one man, Abraham, a nation sprouted and grew. Hundreds of year later a boy was born in the line of Judah, one of Abraham's sons, in the smallest of towns, Bethlehem. His mother Mary wrapped him in swaddling clothes and laid him in a manger.

DIJON MUSTARD

There are several spices (used for flavor or aroma) mentioned in the Bible that we don't use today like myrrh and frankincense. But there are a few others, like mustard that we still used today. In fact, while mustard is one of the oldest spices known to man, more than 700 million pounds of mustard is consumed every year with the most mustard eaten in the United States on pretzels and hot dogs.

While Jesus didn't have hot dogs, he had mustard. For thousands of years, mustard has tasted about the same. Then, in the mid 1800's two men teamed up to create a new mustard flavor. Maurice Grey, who developed a machine to crush and grind mustard seeds, teamed up with August Poupon, who provided money to finance the operation. Together these men created a new mustard flavor by crushing the seeds with the machine and adding a bit of white wine into the mix. The resulting Dijon mustard, named after the town of Dijon France, became a big hit. If you go to the mustard aisle in your grocery store, you can still find this popular Dijon mustard for sale.

Jesus grew up and spread the gospel to the sons and daughters of Abraham. At first, only a handful of disciples followed Jesus, but in a short time that number grew—that tiny seed spread and became a large tree. After Jesus went back to heaven Peter preached to the crowd and 3000 people believed after that one message! All of Jesus's followers became a new family—bound by faith in Jesus, love for God, and love for each other. Abraham was still the father of this new family but now anyone in the whole world who believed in Jesus could be a part of God's family.

What about the birds—who do they represent? The birds are all the nations of the world. God said to Abraham, "through your offspring all nations on earth will be blessed" (Genesis 22:18 NIV). Jesus said, "Come to me, all you who are weary and burdened, and I will give you rest" (Matthew 11:28 NIV).

The Parable of the Leaven is very similar. It shows how one nation (the leaven), affects the whole world (the dough); the gospel starts with one man, Jesus, and spreads to affect the whole earth.

Talk about It

▸ Can you remember what the kingdom of heaven is? *(The kingdom of heaven is simply God's rule and reign over his sons and daughters. Whenever you hear the word* kingdom, *you must remember who the king is. Jesus is the King and we are the people of his kingdom.)*

▸ To what can you compare the mustard seed or the leaven? *(The mustard seed and leaven can be compared to the people of Israel that began with one man Abraham, but grew into a mighty nation of Israel. It can also be compared to the gospel message that spread to all the peoples of the world.)*

▸ Who do the birds represent? *(The birds represent all the different peoples of the earth. If you are not of Jewish descent, which is the mustard tree, then your family is one of the birds in the branches.)*

Pray about It

Thank God for allowing that tiny seed to grow into a great tree so that you and I might find rest in Jesus.

Going Deeper

We talk about Abraham in our lesson this week. God called Abram (his original name) to leave his home for a land that God would show him. Abram obeyed God by faith and moved. God changed his name to Abraham and made a covenant (gave him a promise) that his offspring would grow into a great nation that would bless all the nations of the earth. It was out of the line of Abraham that Jesus was born. Jesus fulfills the promise God made to Abraham to bless all the nations through his seed. Here are some of the key Scriptures from the Old Testament about his life.

The Call of Abraham—"Now the LORD said to Abram, 'Go from your country and your kindred and your father's house to the land that I will show you. And I will make of you a great nation, and I will bless you and make your name great, so that you will be a blessing'" (Genesis 12:1–2).

God's Promise to Abraham—" 'Look toward heaven, and number the stars, if you are able to number them.' Then he said to him, 'So shall your offspring be.' And he believed the LORD, and he counted it to him as righteousness" (Genesis 15:5–6).

God changed his name—"No longer shall your name be called Abram, but your name shall be Abraham, for I have made you the father of a multitude of nations. I will make you exceedingly fruitful, and I will make you into nations, and kings shall come from you. And I will establish my covenant between me and you and your offspring after you throughout their generations for an everlasting covenant, to be God to you and to your offspring after you" (Genesis 17:5–7).

Day Three

Listen Up

Read Matthew 13:34–35:

> *All these things Jesus said to the crowds in parables; indeed, he said nothing to them without a parable. This was to fulfill what was spoken by the prophet: "I will open my mouth in parables; I will utter what has been hidden since the foundation of the world."*

Think about It

In between the Parable of the Leaven and the explanation of the Parable of the Wheat and Weeds, Matthew gives a short but important piece of information. One of the prophets predicted Jesus would teach in parables and these parables would reveal secret information that was "hidden" since the creation of the earth.

Did you hear that? Every time you hold a Bible in your hand you have the answers that people from ages ago searched to find. How excited would you be if you found an old map to a pirate's buried treasure? Or what if you found an old prospector's notes that told you the exact location to his hidden gold mine? Wouldn't you be excited? Well, the Bible holds a richer hidden treasure—the answer to the questions, who is the promised Messiah? How can I live forever? And how can I be saved from my sin? Long ago the prophets foretold a day would come when the secrets, hidden from of old, would be made known. The prophet Asaph gave us an important clue; the secrets would be revealed in parables.

We find the prophecy, written by Asaph, in Psalm 78. It reads, "Give ear, O my people, to my teaching; incline your ears to the words of my mouth! I will open my mouth in a parable; I will utter dark sayings from of old, things that we have heard and known, that our fathers have told us. We will not hide them from their children, but tell to the coming generation the glorious deeds of the LORD, and his might, and the wonders that he has done" (Psalms 78:1–4).

The most glorious of all God's deeds is summarized in John 3:16: "For God so loved the world, that he gave his only Son, that whoever believes in him should not perish but have eternal life."

Talk about It

▶ Who was Asaph? *(Asaph was the prophet who wrote Psalm 78. He also was the chief musician for King David and led the worship with his sons by his side at the dedication of the temple.)*

▶ What has been hidden since the foundation of the world? *(God promised that a future son of Eve would crush the head of Satan. But what folks didn't know was who that deliverer would be. The prophets gave hints but didn't know when he would be born or what his name was. Today we know that Jesus is the one who forgives sin—he is the one who crushed the head of the serpent.)*

▶ What is the most glorious of all the deeds of the Lord? What is the most wonderful thing God ever did? *(The most wonderful and glorious thing God ever did is summed up in John 3:16: "For God so loved the world, that he gave his only Son, that whoever believes in him should not perish but have eternal life.")*

Pray about It

Thank God that you get to know the most important secret in the world—that God sent his Son Jesus to earth to die for our sins so that we could be forgiven.

Going Deeper

Asaph's prophecy comes with an appeal to teach our children about the glorious deeds and wonders of the Lord. Here Asaph hints that the sayings of old can be known and have been passed down for generations. So, what are these dark sayings—the things hidden since the creation of the earth?

We know today that the secret or hidden message is the gospel, which is basically God's plan to save his people from their sin by sending a son of Adam and Eve to deliver them. Remember, after the fall in the Garden of Eden, God said that a future son of Eve would crush the head of the serpent? That part is not so secret and was passed down from father to son. But who that son would be was a mystery. Jesus revealed that he was the Promised One.

By reading the Bible, we know that Jesus was born as a Son of Adam (one of Adam's descendants) to crush the head of Satan by dying on the cross for our sins. That's the most glorious deed of the Lord and the most wonderful thing he has done. The prophets longed to see the child of promise but died before Jesus was born (Matthew 13:17). Today, we look back at the parables and realize the hidden information that they reveal is that Jesus is the Messiah, the promised deliverer who can save us from the curse of sin.

Day Four

Listen Up

Read Matthew 13:44–46:

> *"The kingdom of heaven is like treasure hidden in a field, which a man found and covered up. Then in his joy he goes and sells all that he has and buys that field.*
>
> *"Again, the kingdom of heaven is like a merchant in search of fine pearls, who, on finding one pearl of great value, went and sold all that he had and bought it."*

Think about It

The Parable of the Hidden Treasure and the Parable of the Pearl of Great Price form another pair in the thirteenth chapter of Matthew's gospel. Both parables present the same truth. The kingdom of heaven is priceless, worth more than all your possessions. If you discovered a treasure map to a pirate's hidden treasure but didn't know what it was, you might just throw it away. In the same way, many people read these two parables and just throw them away. They don't realize, that hidden in these two stories is the greatest treasure of all time, Jesus.

One man discovers a treasure, hidden in a field. He knows that if he takes the treasure out of the field and it is discovered that it came from a certain field, the owner of the field could lay claim and say, "The treasure is mine, give it back to me." What does the man who finds it do? He sells everything he owns and buys the field. Once the field is his, so is the treasure. The second man, a merchant also finds a treasure; a single pearl worth more than all the pearls he has ever collected. The merchant sells all he has to buy the pearl. He sells every pearl in his collection, he sells his ship, and he sells his business. Like the man who discovered the treasure in the field he sells everything he owns and buys the one precious pearl of great value.

What do the pearl and the treasure represent? The simple answer of course is the kingdom of heaven. But more specifically, the pearl and the treasure represent the King of the kingdom—Jesus Christ and the salvation he offers to all people who place their trust in him. Jesus is our treasure and is worth more than all the silver and gold and all the pearls of the world. And yet, you can't buy Jesus, he offers himself to you; he offers his salvation to you, for free.

The pearl of great price and the treasure of the field are free for us to take. Sadly, people don't realize the wonderful treasure we have in Jesus. Rather than believe in Jesus they look to find their treasure in the things of the world. But Jesus warned, "For what does it profit a man to gain the whole world and forfeit his soul?" (Mark 8:36).

Talk about It

▶ What do the treasure in the field, the pearl, the merchant, and the man who discovers the treasure represent? *(Jesus is the treasure in the field and the pearl of great price. The man who discovers the treasure and the merchant who finds the pearl represent us discovering Jesus.)*

▶ If the treasure is Jesus, does that mean we need to sell all that we own to buy Jesus? *(Of course you cannot "buy" Jesus, but you can give up everything that stands in the way of believing and trusting in him. We need to be willing to give up anything that seeks to draw our love away from God. Once Jesus told a young man to sell all that he had and come and follow him. The man walked away sad, for he was very rich. He chose his treasure over Jesus. You can read the story in Matthew 19:16–22.)*

▶ Why is Jesus our greatest treasure? *(Parents, draw out your children here to see what they know. Jesus is our greatest treasure because he willingly gave up his life for us to take our punishment upon the cross, then rose again in victory over death, that we too might live forever in heaven. Jesus offers us the free gift of salvation if we believe in him and turn away from our sin. Imagine a medicine that could cure every sickness. How valuable would a small vial of that medicine be to a person who is dying of a terrible disease? Surely we would sell all that we had to buy the medicine. Jesus is our healer, and provides our forgiveness. Those who believe in him will never die, but live forever in heaven with God. You just can't get more valuable than that.)*

Pray about It

Pray that God would help you value Jesus more than everything else in the world.

Going Deeper

The prophet Isaiah foretold of a free salvation when he said, "Come, everyone who thirsts, come to the waters; and he who has no money, come, buy and eat! Come, buy wine and milk without money and without price" (Isaiah 55:1). Jesus told the woman at the well that he could give her a drink so satisfying she would never be thirsty again (John 4:14). Jesus also told the crowds, "I am the bread of life; whoever comes to me shall not hunger, and whoever believes in me shall never thirst" (John 6:35).

Even though Jesus taught that our salvation is free, it does cost us everything. We can't earn our way to Jesus by giving up everything, but faith in Jesus does require we place Jesus first before everything. While we may at times feel the need to always balance one of these truths with the other, the Bible doesn't present them that way.

> "To the thirsty I will give from the spring of the water of life without payment." (Revelation 21:6 which is Jesus quoting from Isaiah 55:1)
>
> "But the free gift is not like the trespass. For if many died through one man's trespass, much more have the grace of God and the free gift by the grace of that one man Jesus Christ abounded for many." (Romans 5:15)
>
> "Any one of you who does not renounce all that he has cannot be my disciple." (Luke 14:33)
>
> "If anyone would come after me, let him deny himself and take up his cross and follow me." (Matthew 16:24)

Listen Up

Read Matthew 13:47–52:

> *"Again, the kingdom of heaven is like a net that was thrown into the sea and gathered fish of every kind. When it was full, men drew it ashore and sat down and sorted the good into containers but threw away the bad. So it will be at the end of the age. The angels will come out and separate the evil from the righteous and throw them into the fiery furnace. In that place there will be weeping and gnashing of teeth.*
>
> *"Have you understood all these things?" They said to him, "Yes." And he said to them, "Therefore every scribe who has been trained for the kingdom of heaven is like a master of a house, who brings out of his treasure what is new and what is old."*

Think about It

After sharing the Parable of the Fish Net, Jesus asked the disciples if they understood what he was teaching. They had the benefit of already hearing the explanation of the Parable of the Wheat and the Weeds and could see the Parable of the Fish Net was very similar. It also helped that they were fisherman, so they knew all about fishing. They also likely remembered Jesus saying he would make them fishers of men (Matthew 4:19).

The fish in the parable represent all people, both believers and unbelievers much like the wheat and the weeds. The net is God's judgment that will eventually catch every person in the world. Until then, believers and unbelievers live together in their neighborhoods, and in the church (the sea). Think about the disciples, Jesus drew eleven faithful disciples (the good fish), but he also drew in Judas who betrayed him (the bad fish). Judas seemed to fit in, but deep in his heart he didn't love Jesus, he was stealing from him (John 12:6).

One day, each of us will be gathered in by God's great judgment net and he will separate the righteous (good fish) and the unrighteous (bad fish).

That's why we can't just pretend to treasure Jesus. Some people say that they love Jesus but because their heart is not changed, they don't always live for Jesus. People can go to church on Sunday, put on their best clothes and act nice to everyone around them, but not really love Jesus in their heart. Treasuring Jesus is not just about the words we say, or how good we look on Sunday. Treasuring Jesus is about what's inside your heart; do you really love Jesus and want to live for him? The crazy part is that none of us would love Jesus if he didn't change our hearts of stone and open our eyes to see how wonderful he is. The parable warns us that one day, the giant net of God's judgment is going to come and catch us all. But only those who truly love the Lord will be spared.

Talk about It

▶ How is the Parable of the Fish Net like the Parable of the Wheat and the Weeds? *(Parents, review the parables and help the children make the connections like the good fish are like the wheat and the bad fish like the weeds. The fishermen dragging in the net are like the servants of the master.)*

▶ What did Matthew do that helps us to know he listened carefully to Jesus's teaching? *(Matthew is the apostle who wrote the gospel that we are reading so we know he paid close attention to what Jesus said.)*

▶ Which of the parables we studied this week did you enjoy the most? *(Parents, draw out your children and help them to see that the stories and lessons in the Bible are meant to touch our lives. Share which of the parables most affected you.)*

Pray about It

Thank God for giving us the parables so that we can learn more about him and his kingdom.

Going Deeper

A scribe in Jesus day made copies of the Bible, but he also taught the Scriptures. Pastors today are like the scribes Jesus referred to, who teach the people about the kingdom of heaven. Jesus said the disciples would be like a master of a house showing off treasure, both old and new. The old treasures are the stories that point to Jesus. Every lamb sacrificed in the Old Testament points forward to Jesus, the Lamb of God who takes away our sins. The new treasure includes Jesus and his teachings, particularly the parables that he shared with his disciples. Matthew took Jesus's charge very seriously and recorded the parables for our benefit.

Week 4

The Good Shepherd

Let's Look at the Week. . .

When the Apostle John wrote his gospel, he did not include the longer parables of Jesus. But it you read carefully, you will discover short mini parables that are nearly hidden in the text. In John 12:24 for example, Jesus says, "unless a grain of wheat falls into the earth and dies, it remains alone; but if it dies, it bears much fruit." While John doesn't call this short illustration a parable, Jesus used these brief word picture illustrations in his teaching much like he did the longer parables found in the other gospels.

In addition to these short illustrations, John also records longer word pictures called, figures of speech. For example, Jesus said that he was the vine and his followers are branches on the vine. That doesn't literally mean the Son of God is a walking grapevine with branches sticking out of himself. The word picture is designed to help us understand that as "branches" we get everything we need from the vine. If you cut a branch off the vine, it dies. In a similar way, our only hope for eternal life is to be connected to Jesus.

This week we'll examine the most well known of Jesus's word pictures, The Good Shepherd. It is the longest and best example of a figure of speech in Jesus's teaching. This wonderful picture of a shepherd caring for his sheep helps us better understand and appreciate God and his care for us.

Get Ready

The action word of the week is follow.

The word *follow* means to go after someone or something. If you follow a butterfly into the woods, you observe and track its movements so that you don't lose sight of it. If you follow your dog around the house, you walk on the same path he walks.

We can also follow instructions. Following instructions means we obey the directions for each step we read. Sometimes when you get a new game or toy you must first follow the instructions to learn how to play or how to put it together.

Sometimes we follow people. We follow our parents a lot. They take us everywhere and expect that we won't wander away. We follow our teachers' instructions in school. When they tell us to open to page thirty-five, we follow their direction and open our books to page thirty-five.

This week we will learn that Jesus is the most important person to follow. The teaching Jesus gave us in the Bible is the most important instruction we will ever learn.

Name the Sheep

(The purpose of this activity is to better understand the role of a shepherd.)

Supplies:

- Access to the Internet and a printer (or photos from a magazine)

Search the Internet for an image of up to five sheep standing in a group. Print the photo and then gather your children. Explain to the children that a good shepherd names all the sheep in his flock and calls them each by name. Some Middle Eastern shepherds today still care for more than 200 sheep. They name their sheep from birth and can tell you the name of each one. Often the sheep are named by some physical characteristic like "Fluffy Ears" or "Big Eyes." Or the sheep may be named after the place or time of their birth, such as "Daisy" or "Hillside."

Take a look at your sheep photo and play the role of a shepherd and come up with a different name for each of the sheep in your flock.

Day One

Listen Up

Read John 10:1–6:

> *"Truly, truly, I say to you, he who does not enter the sheepfold by the door but climbs in by another way, that man is a thief and a robber. But he who enters by the door is the shepherd of the sheep. To him the gatekeeper opens.*

The sheep hear his voice, and he calls his own sheep by name and leads them out. When he has brought out all his own, he goes before them, and the sheep follow him, for they know his voice. A stranger they will not follow, but they will flee from him, for they do not know the voice of strangers." This figure of speech Jesus used with them, but they did not understand what he was saying to them.

Think about It

Jesus used the figure of speech of a shepherd and sheep to describe his relationship with us, his followers. Jesus is the shepherd and we are the sheep.

Jesus used an accurate description of the way a real shepherd of Palestine cared for and lead his sheep in and out of the sheepfold. The people of Israel were very familiar with raising sheep, so this word picture was filled with meaning for them. But few people who read the Bible today know much about caring for sheep. When we think of sheepfold, for example, we probably picture a large barn with several doors in and out. But in Jesus day, a sheepfold was likely only a stone wall, with a single gate opening. The wall helped to protect the sheep from attacks in all directions. Any wolves or thieves planning to snatch the sheep up in the night would have to go through the shepherd who stood watch at the opening.

The elements of this word picture, like the parables Jesus taught represent real life people and things. The sheepfold is the church. Like a real sheepfold, there is only one way in, you must enter by way of the shepherd. The only way the shepherd is going to let you in is if you are a part of the flock. The sheep are the people in the church who become a part of the flock when they believe in Jesus and follow his voice.

Now when the disciples heard this figure of speech, much like the parables, they didn't understand what Jesus was talking about. Imagine if you go up to your friends and said, "Hey guys, did you know that he who does not enter the sheepfold by the door but climbs in by another way, that man is a thief and a robber?" Your friends would say, "What in the world are you talking about?" "Why are you talking to us about sheep?" Also, while shepherds were common in Jerusalem, Jesus's disciples were made up of mostly fisherman and one tax collector—so they were not thinking about sheep. Jesus had to explain what he was talking about, but we'll cover that in our next devotion.

Talk about It

▶ What is a figure of speech? *(A figure of speech is a word picture, much like a parable, used to help us understand an important truth. Jesus compared himself to a shepherd, a vine, and a bridegroom to help us understand his relationship to us.)*

▶ Who do the shepherd, the sheep, and the sheepfold represent? *(Jesus is the shepherd, those who believe in him are the sheep, and the sheepfold is the church or family of God.)*

▶ What does the shepherd do to care for the sheep? *(He names them, knows them, leads them into the sheepfold, and protects them at night.)*

Pray about It

Thank Jesus for knowing each of us by name and ask him to help you put your faith and trust in him.

Going Deeper

When Jesus said, "he who does not enter the sheepfold by the door but climbs in by another way, that man is a thief and a robber" (John 10:1), he set Christianity apart as the only path to heaven. In John 14:6 Jesus made this clear, saying, "I am the way, and the truth, and the life. No one comes to the Father except through me."

Other religions, like Islam, Mormonism, and Hinduism believe Jesus existed and was a real person. Islam even teaches Jesus was born of a virgin, ascended into heaven, and will come again. But Islam also denies that Jesus died on the cross, rose again from the dead, and is God the Son. Most importantly, no other religion believes that Jesus is "the only way" to the Father. No other world religion believes Jesus is God the Son who came down as a substitute to die on the cross for the sins of those who would believe.

While Christians are criticized for our narrow-mindedness in saying, "our religion is the only way to get to heaven," we are only repeating the single most fundamental truth of our faith. That is, the sacrifice of Jesus upon the cross for our sin is the only way anyone can have their sin removed. If you remove the cross from Christianity, you simply do not have Christianity. That's why Jesus said that anyone who tries to get in apart from the door is a thief and a robber.

Day Two

Listen Up

Read John 10:7–13:

> *So Jesus again said to them, "Truly, truly, I say to you, I am the door of the sheep. All who came before me are thieves and robbers, but the sheep did not listen to them. I am the door. If anyone enters by me, he will be saved and will go in and out and find pasture. The thief comes only to steal and kill and destroy. I came that they may have life and have it abundantly. I am the good shepherd. The good shepherd lays down his life for the sheep. He who is*

a hired hand and not a shepherd, who does not own the sheep, sees the wolf coming and leaves the sheep and flees, and the wolf snatches them and scatters them. He flees because he is a hired hand and cares nothing for the sheep.

Think about It

In our last devotion, we saw that the disciples didn't understand the shepherd/sheep word picture Jesus used. So here, Jesus included an explanation as he expands the word picture. The disciples discovered that Jesus was teaching about his own ministry and his care for the people of God. Jesus is the Good Shepherd and his followers, the sheep.

Picture a sheepfold with a stone wall and a single open doorway that has no door. Once the shepherd stands in the opening he becomes the defender or door to the sheepfold. With the shepherd standing at the door, the sheep can rest confident they are safe.

We are the sheep who trust in the shepherd, who listen and follow his voice and are saved inside the sheepfold. Jesus is the Good Shepherd who stands by the sheep to protect them when danger comes. Consider some ways in which we can run to Jesus and trust his help and protection.

When we tell a lie, steal something, or fall into some other sin, we can run to Jesus to confess our sin and he will forgive us.

When we ourselves or someone we love becomes sick, we can run to Jesus and ask him to bring healing.

When we have a friend who doesn't believe in Jesus, we can ask Jesus to send his Spirit to open our friend's eyes to the truth.

When we need his help, Jesus doesn't run away. What a comfort this is for us when we go through challenges in life. We can remember Jesus is like a shepherd who stands against thieves and wolves that come to steal, kill, and destroy. This doesn't mean God always answers our prayers the way we want, but we can be certain that Jesus hears our prayers and always stands at the ready to help us.

1. Sheep have rectangular pupils and can see behind themselves without turning their heads.
2. There are more than 1,000,000,000 sheep in the world.
3. One fleece, the wool from one sheep, can spin a fine strand that is 50 miles long.
4. You can scare a sheep to death. If a dog corners a sheep, the sheep can die of the resulting stress.
5. New Zealand has three times as many sheep as it has people.
6. It takes about a pound and a half of wool to make a sweater. Sheep grow between 3 to 30 pounds of wool each year, resulting in 2 to 20 sweaters per sheep.
7. Lost sheep that are found years later, have yielded 90 pounds of wool. That is 60 sweaters worth of wool.
8. Sheep can recognize each other's faces and remember them for years.
9. Wool naturally comes in white, black, grey, brown, and red.
10. The fatty grease that keeps a sheep's wool dry is called lanolin and it is an ingredient in cosmetics. The next time you see a lady put on lipstick, she probably doesn't realize she's smiling with colored wool grease!

Talk about It

▶ Who does Jesus say is the shepherd? Who are the sheep? Who is the thief? *(Jesus said he was the shepherd and we are the sheep, and Satan is the thief and robber looking to steal us away from God.)*

▶ What must the sheep do to be protected by the shepherd? *(The sheep must listen and follow the shepherd. All they have to do to be protected is follow his voice.)*

▶ What do we need to do as sheep to follow Jesus our shepherd? *(We need to listen to his voice and follow him. Jesus calls us to believe in him and place our trust for salvation in his death and resurrection.)*

Pray about It

Thank Jesus for calling us into his sheepfold and for protecting us as our Good Shepherd.

Going Deeper

When Jesus describes himself as the Good Shepherd who cares for the sheep, he is contrasting himself to the leaders of Israel who failed to care for the sheep. Jesus succeeded where Israel failed to care for the sheep, the people of God. Consider the judgment of God as spoken by the prophet Ezekiel:

> "The word of the LORD came to me: "Son of man, prophesy against the shepherds of Israel; prophesy, and say to them, even to the shepherds, Thus says the Lord God: Ah, shepherds of Israel who have been feeding yourselves! Should not shepherds feed the sheep? You eat the fat, you clothe yourselves with the wool, you slaughter the fat ones, but you do not feed the sheep. The weak you have not strengthened, the sick you have not healed, the injured you have not bound up, the strayed you have not brought back, the lost you have not sought, and with force and harshness you have ruled them. So they were scattered, because there was no shepherd, and they became food for all the wild beasts. My sheep were scattered; they wandered over all the mountains and on every high hill. My sheep were scattered over all the face of the earth, with none to search or seek for them." (Ezekiel 34:1–6)

In today's Bible passage, we see that Jesus succeeded where the leaders of Israel failed to care for God's flock. Jesus was the shepherd who was so dedicated to the sheep that he was willing to give up his life. That's a picture of what Jesus did for us on the cross. Jesus gave up his life for us, taking the punishment we deserved. He did this to conquer the enemies of sin and death and to free us from Satan's grip. Now, everyone who trusts in Jesus enters into his sheepfold, the family of God and receives eternal life. Jesus said he would never lose a single one of God's children (John 6:37–39). Once again, where the leaders of Israel failed, Jesus prevailed.

Day Three

Listen Up

Read John 10:14–21:

> *I am the good shepherd. I know my own and my own know me, just as the Father knows me and I know the Father; and I lay down my life for the sheep. And I have other sheep that are not of this fold. I must bring them also, and they will listen to my voice. So there will be one flock, one shepherd. For this reason the Father loves me, because I lay down my life that I may take it up again. No one takes it from me, but I lay it down of my own accord. I have authority to lay it down, and I have authority to take it up again. This charge I have received from my Father."*
>
> *There was again a division among the Jews because of these words. Many of them said, "He has a demon, and is insane; why listen to him?" Others said, "These are not the words of one who is oppressed by a demon. Can a demon open the eyes of the blind?"*

Think about It

Did you ever go to a crowded place, like the beach or a carnival and wander a bit away from your mom and dad without knowing? Everyone around you is talking, some people are shouting and there is a lot of background noise. But once your mom or dad realize you have wandered away, they shout your name. Without even thinking, your head snaps back the moment you hear their call. Ten other parents might also be calling their children but you wouldn't turn toward them. You recognize your own mom or dad's voice and turn without thinking about it. That's what happens when Jesus calls his sheep. At the sound of his voice, his children respond. But not everyone Jesus taught recognized his voice.

Not everyone who heard Jesus speak believed in him. They thought he was crazy, or worse, that he was possessed by a demon.

In another part of the Bible, Jesus revealed the reason—they were not a part of his family. Read the account in John 8:42–45:

> *Jesus said to them, "If God were your Father, you would love me, for I came from God and I am here. I came not of my own accord, but he sent me. Why do you not understand what I say? It is because you cannot bear to hear my word. You are of your father the devil, and your will is to do your father's desires. He was a murderer from the beginning, and does not stand in the truth, because there is no truth in him. When he lies, he speaks out of his own character, for he is a liar and the father of lies. But because I tell the truth, you do not believe me."*

Looking back on his words, it is essential for us to hear the important message he is sharing. When Jesus said, "I lay down my life for the sheep," do you also hear him referring to his death on the cross and the forgiveness of sins? When he said, "I lay down my life that I may take it up again," can you hear him say, "I am going to rise again?" Those who have ears to hear, understand that Jesus came to conquer sin and death. Everyone who hears and places their trust in Jesus will be forgiven and share life forever with Jesus in heaven.

Now the real question is, can you hear the voice of Jesus calling, saying that he died for you?

Talk about It

▶ How did the crowd respond to Jesus's teaching? *(Some believed but others thought he was crazy or that he was possessed by a demon.)*

▶ What helped the people believe? *(They saw Jesus do miracles, like give sight to the blind.)*

▶ What about today? Do we still have the same choice—to hear his voice—to believe or reject Jesus? *(Yes, today everyone has the same choice. Some will believe that Jesus is the Son of God who died on the cross for our sins and others will reject him and refuse to believe. The question for all of us is, what will we do?)*

Pray about It

Ask God to pour out his Holy Spirit upon each person in your family to give you the grace to believe in Jesus.

Going Deeper

The flock is the people of God. They are the sheep of his fold. When Jesus came to this earth, he first came to the Jews. They were God's people. The Gentiles were not a part of God's flock.

But Jesus came to fulfill the promise he gave to Abraham to bless all the nations of the earth through him (Genesis 22:18). Now all who believe in Jesus become a part of the family of Abraham and heirs of the promise of God. The Apostle Paul said, "For as many of you as were baptized into Christ have put on Christ. There is neither Jew nor Greek, there is neither slave nor free, there is no male and female, for you are all one in Christ Jesus. And if you are Christ's, then you are Abraham's offspring, heirs according to promise" (Galatians 3:27–29).

Day Four

Listen Up

Read John 10:22–30:

> *At that time the Feast of Dedication took place at Jerusalem. It was winter, and Jesus was walking in the temple, in the colonnade of Solomon. So the Jews gathered around him and said to him, "How long will you keep us in suspense? If you are the Christ, tell us plainly." Jesus answered them, "I told you, and you do not believe. The works that I do in my Father's name bear witness about me, but you do not believe because you are not among my sheep. My sheep hear my voice, and I know them, and they follow me. I give them eternal life, and they will*

> *never perish, and no one will snatch them out of my hand. My Father, who has given them to me, is greater than all, and no one is able to snatch them out of the Father's hand. I and the Father are one."*

Think about It

If you were to venture out to a field with a shepherd and his flock, you could see firsthand how amazingly a shepherd can call his sheep. They actually know his voice. You or a friend could call out to the sheep and say, "Hey sheep, come to me," and they would ignore you and keep chomping on the grass as though you didn't say a word. But, when the shepherd calls out to the sheep they instantly stop eating, perk up their heads and look in his direction. With the second call they start moving toward him, and by the third call have started to run, not just one but the entire flock—sometimes as many as one hundred sheep, all obeying the voice of the shepherd. It is an amazing sight to see. When the sheep hear the shepherd's voice they stop what they are doing and come.

Since most of us don't live around sheep, we don't realize that sheep come just as quickly as our pet dog comes when he hears our voice. The Jews who were questioning Jesus didn't believe. They didn't want to come to Jesus. They didn't believe he was the Son of God. They didn't believe he was the Messiah come to deliver them. Jesus could see they were not responding to his teaching and used the picture of shepherd/sheep to correct them.

What about you? Do you believe when you hear the words of Jesus? Are you one of his sheep? Everyone who hears the words of Jesus and believes that he is the Son of God, sent to take away our sins, is like a sheep hearing the voice of the shepherd. Everyone who then runs to Jesus for the forgiveness of their sins is like the sheep who come to the shepherd. Jesus said, "All that the Father gives me will come to me, and whoever comes to me I will never cast out" (John 6:37). This means that everyone who hears his voice and comes to him is welcomed into the flock (or family) of God.

Talk about It

▶ What did Jesus say he would do for the sheep who hear his voice? *(Jesus said he would give them eternal life and nobody would be able to snatch them out of his hand.)*

▶ What does Jesus mean by saying he gives them eternal life? *(The word* eternal *means forever. One day all those who believe and place their trust in Jesus will live forever with him and nothing will be able to take us away.)*

▶ What did Jesus mean when he said, "I and the Father are one?" *(Our one God is made up of three distinct persons—Father, Son, and Holy Spirit. While Jesus and the Father are two distinct persons, they are also one. It is hard for us to understand how two can be one. God is amazing and greater than our minds can comprehend.)*

Pray about It

Ask Jesus to help you hear his voice and follow him so that you can live with him in heaven for all eternity.

Going Deeper

The Jews grew tired of listening to Jesus speak in confusing parables. So they asked Jesus to tell them plainly if he was the Christ—the one God would send to deliver Israel. If Jesus said, "I am the Messiah"—the Jews would think he was the one to lead a revolt against Rome—they already tried to make him king. You see the Jews were looking for a Messiah to lead an army and set them free from the rule of the Roman Empire. But if Jesus said, "No, I am not the Messiah you are looking for," he would deny the truth, for he was indeed the Messiah. So Jesus answered them, "I told you, and you do not believe. The works that I do in my Father's name bear witness about me, but you do not believe because you are not among my sheep."

The problem is that many of the Jews were not a part of God's flock. The truth of Jesus was hidden from them. The parables and figures of speech Jesus taught only frustrated them. As we learned in our last devotion, they did not recognize his voice calling them. They were not interested in learning from Jesus. They were only interested in hearing what they wanted. But for those who were drawn to Jesus then and for us today, Jesus's words bring great comfort. The sheep (those who believe and trust in Jesus) are safe with him. If you believe, he will give you eternal life and no one can ever take you away from Jesus. He will protect you for eternity.

While Jesus didn't stand up and say, "I am the Messiah," he did tell them he was God. Jesus said he and the Father were one. We will see in our next devotion that only made them angrier.

Day Five

Listen Up

Read John 10:31–33:

> *The Jews picked up stones again to stone him. Jesus answered them, "I have shown you many good works from the Father; for which of them are you going to stone me?" The Jews answered him, "It is not for a good work that we are going to stone you but for blasphemy, because you, being a man, make yourself God."*

Think about It

The Jews may not have understood the shepherd/sheep figure of speech that Jesus was using to teach, but they did understand Jesus's answer to their question. They asked him if he was the Messiah and Jesus replied by telling them that he was God. Some people say that Jesus was just a good teacher and that he never claimed to be God. But here, in John's gospel it is plain to see that Jesus in fact did say he was God. Sadly, the Jews did not believe. In verse 39 we see that the Jews tried then to arrest Jesus but, because it was not yet time for him to die, he simply escaped from their grasp.

When the Jews heard Jesus say, "I and the Father are one" (John 10:30), they got angry. The penalty for anyone mocking or insulting God was death by stoning. Since they did not believe Jesus, they picked up stones to kill him.

Jesus challenged them and reminded them of the miracles he performed. The Jews had seen Jesus give sight to the blind and heal the lame. Jesus asked them to explain for which of those good works they going to stone him.

Talk about It

▸ What did Jesus say in verse 30 that made the Jews so angry? *(We learned in our last devotion that Jesus said he and God the Father were one, meaning that he was God.)*

▸ What were the Jews planning to do with the stones? *(They were planning to throw them at Jesus to kill him.)*

▸ We have the same choice: do we trust Jesus or reject him? Why do you think people refuse to believe? *(People don't believe because they don't want to follow Jesus. They want to live life independently and not be told what to do. Therefore, they reject God and live for themselves.)*

Pray about It

Take time to pray for the members of your family and ask God to give each one grace to believe and follow the words of Jesus that they too can spend eternity with him.

Going Deeper

There is another passage in the gospel of John where Jesus claimed to be God. In John 8:48–59, the Jews accused Jesus of being possessed by demons for saying that those who kept his word would not taste death. They confronted him, "Are you greater than our father Abraham, who died?" Jesus answered saying that even Abraham rejoiced to see him. They mocked Jesus saying that he was less than fifty years old, how could he have seen Abraham? That's when Jesus made the claim, "before Abraham was, I am" (John 8:58). The Jews immediately turned to stone Jesus, for they understood he was claiming to be God. You see, when Moses asked God what his name was, God answered saying that his name was "I am." The same words Jesus quoted.

Week 5

Do I Have to Forgive?

Let's Look at the Week. . .

While we all use the word *forgive*, not everyone understands what the word forgive actually means. Some think that in order to grant forgiveness, you must forget what the person did against you. Others believe you must wait to extend forgiveness until the person who hurt you is truly sorry. Others ask for forgiveness as a way to end an argument or problem, without truly thinking much about what they've done. If someone were to ask you, "What does forgiveness mean and in what circumstances should you extend forgiveness to others?" how would you answer?

This week we will study the parables Jesus used to teach forgiveness. We'll begin our week of devotions looking at the Parable of the Unmerciful Servant, which uses the forgiveness of a debt to help us understand what forgiveness means. Jesus knew that this example would be one of the best ways to help someone understand the meaning of forgiveness.

We will also explore Jesus's death on the cross and how it equips us to extend forgiveness to others. We will finish our week looking at the word picture of the Mustard Seed of Faith. You may be surprised to find out that it too is connected to our theme of forgiveness.

Get Ready

The action word of the week is forgive.

Forgive is a word we use when we cancel a debt or set a person free from a penalty. Imagine going to the store with your mom and dad and you see a candy bar you want to buy, but you left your money at home. To purchase the candy, you need your parents to loan you the money. Perhaps you say, "Mom, can I get some candy, I'll pay you back when we get home." If your mom agrees and loans you the money to buy the candy, you become indebted to your mom; you owe her money.

Now imagine that when you get home, you run to your room and scoop up the loose change on your dresser and offer your mom a fist full of pennies. When your mom sees the coins, she realizes that you don't have enough money and says, "You keep your pennies; there's no need to pay me back." Wow, you owed your mom a debt, but she forgave it. She paid your debt.

If the police catch you speeding, they can give you a ticket that costs you money. But sometimes, if you go to the local judge and ask for mercy, he will forgive your penalty and give you a second chance. If the judge says, "not guilty," then your fine is removed and you are set free from the penalty of the ticket.

This week we will study the parables Jesus used to teach about forgiveness. We will learn how God forgave us and how we should forgive others. Forgiveness is one of the most important action words we will learn.

Robber Robber

(This activity will help your children grasp the concept of forgiveness.)

Supplies:

- Gummy bears, candy or fruit chews

Make a pile of gummy bears on the table—two gummy bears for each child and two for you. (If you have two children you would put six gummy bears in the pile.) Gather your children around and tell them this story.

One day a mom (or change this to dad) gathered her children around the table to give each of them two gummy bears. One of the children became so excited that he grabbed three gummy bears and popped them into his mouth. (Now give three gummy bears to one of your children and tell them to pretend they are the child from the story and pop the gummy bears into his mouth.)

The mom corrected her child for taking three gummy bears, but now there was a problem. When she passed out the remaining bears, she was one gummy bear short. When she started, there were only enough gummy bears for each person to have two.

The child who gobbled up the three gummy bears was sorry and asked his mom to forgive him. His mom graciously forgave her son, but there was a cost to bear. Instead of taking two gummy bears for herself, she only took one so the other children could each have two.

There is always a cost with forgiveness. Even though the child in our story was sorry and asked his mom to forgive him, his apology could not bring back the gummy bear he ate. Someone had to bear the cost. In this case, the mom bore the cost by taking one less gummy bear.

Day One

Listen Up

Read Matthew 18:21–30:

> *Then Peter came up and said to him, "Lord, how often will my brother sin against me, and I forgive him? As many as seven times?" Jesus said to him, "I do not say to you seven times, but seventy-seven times.*
>
> *"Therefore the kingdom of heaven may be compared to a king who wished to settle accounts with his servants. When he began to settle, one was brought to him who owed him ten thousand talents. And since he could not pay, his master ordered him to be sold, with his wife and children and all that he had, and payment to be made. So the servant fell on his knees, imploring him, 'Have patience with me, and I will pay you everything.' And out of pity for him, the master of that servant released him and forgave him the debt. But when that same servant went out, he found one of his fellow servants who owed him a hundred denarii, and seizing him, he began to choke him, saying, 'Pay what you owe.' So his fellow servant fell down and pleaded with him, 'Have patience with me, and I will pay you.' He refused and went and put him in prison until he should pay the debt.*

Think about It

Can you think of a time when somebody was unkind toward you? Has anyone ever broken your favorite toy, or lied to you, or said something unkind? What if that same friend apologized but the next time he came over to your house, he did the same thing again? Would you have to forgive him again? What if he came to your house on Monday and lied; came to your house Tuesday and said something mean; came to your house on Wednesday and pushed you down; then came to your house on Thursday and said he was sorry. Would you still have to forgive your friend after sinning against you so many days in a row? That's what Peter wanted to know from Jesus. How many times do must we forgive? To answer Peter Jesus told him the Parable of the Unforgiving Servant.

The king in the parable forgives one of his servants an enormous debt; one that he could never repay—ten thousand talents (see the fun fact to learn how much this is). That same guy, free of his debt against the king, approached a fellow servant who owed him money. Rather than allow the king's kindness to soften his heart and forgive his fellow servant, he demanded repayment. When the fellow servant couldn't come up with the money, the first servant had him thrown in prison.

Who do the characters in the parable represent? We should begin by comparing ourselves to the first servant in the parable. Each of us has a great unpayable debt of sin against God (the king). Through Jesus, God provided each of us with a way to have our debt cancelled. If we turn from our sin, and place our trust in Jesus, we can be forgiven of our debt against God.

Once our sin is forgiven, the question for us becomes, how will we treat those who sin against us? Will God's mercy toward us soften our hearts so that we are willing to forgive those who sin against us? Or, will we act like the ungrateful servant and demand a payment from them?

It is also very important to remember that as Christians, we will continue to sin. In fact, we sin every day of the week. We sin on Monday, Tuesday, Wednesday, Thursday, Friday, Saturday, and Sunday. Even then, God never stops forgiving us. God continues to offer forgiveness to his children who place their faith in him. If God forgives and then keeps on forgiving us, we should do the same for others.

A talent is a measure of weight from biblical times, equal to around 80 pounds. You could have a talent of gold, silver, or bronze. One talent of silver (80 pounds of silver) would be a solid 6-inch cube or about 216 cubic inches (one-eighth of a cubic foot). Ten thousand talents of silver (the amount owed by the first servant) would occupy approximately 1,250 cubic feet of space. If an adult elephant occupies about 150 cubic feet of space, ten thousand talents of silver would occupy the space of about eight elephants. If silver has a value of $20 per ounce, one talent (1,280 ounces) would be worth about $25,600. That would make each of the solid silver elephants worth approximately $30.6 million.

Talk about It

▸ Why did Peter ask how many times he was required to forgive? *(Peter wanted to know the limit so that once a person crossed the limit he would not have to forgive them.)*

▸ Have you ever experienced a time when it was difficult to forgive another person? *(Parents, help your children remember a time when they got into a fight or argument with their siblings and found it challenging to forgive.)*

▸ What did God do for us that should encourage us to forgive those who sin against us? *(God paid our great unpayable debt. In order to forgive us for our sin, God sent his Son Jesus to take the punishment we deserved. When Jesus hung on the cross, God the Father poured out upon him, the punishment we deserved. That's how Jesus paid our debt. Remembering what Jesus did for us, can help us want to forgive others. By reinforcing this with your children you can help them see the connection between God's mercy toward us and the mercy we can extend to others. Help your children think of things they need to forgive more than once, like when their sibling or friends don't share.)*

Pray about It

Ask God to help you forgive those who sin against you.

Going Deeper

To better understand the parable of the Unforgiving Servant it is important to study the context. The Parable of the Unforgiving Servant comes after the first part of Matthew 18 where Jesus was teaching his disciples the proper way to correct someone for sinning. It was in the midst of this teaching that Peter asked his question about forgiveness. He wanted to know how many times he must forgive someone who repeatedly does sins against you.

Peter wanted to know, when was enough, enough—when can he finally say to a person, "That's it, you've gone too far, you've sinned against me one too many times, I will not forgive you again." Is it ever OK not to forgive? In reply to Peter's question, Jesus tells the Parable of the Unforgiving Servant.

Day Two

Listen Up

Read Matthew 18:31–35:

> *When his fellow servants saw what had taken place, they were greatly distressed, and they went and reported to their master all that had taken place. Then his master*

> *summoned him and said to him, 'You wicked servant! I forgave you all that debt because you pleaded with me. And should not you have had mercy on your fellow servant, as I had mercy on you?' And in anger his master delivered him to the jailers, until he should pay all his debt. So also my heavenly Father will do to every one of you, if you do not forgive your brother from your heart."*

Think about It

When people read a parable like The Unforgiving Servant, they usually identify with one of the characters of the story. So, when you read about the man who discovered a treasure in the field, you might think, "I wish I could discover a treasure like that guy." In that example, you are comparing yourself to the man who discovered the treasure. In most cases, we like to see ourselves as the good character in the story.

Who did you compare yourself to in our parable today? Most readers compare themselves with the king (master) and join him in looking down at the wicked servant. Did you think to yourself, "That was incredibly selfish of the servant to withhold forgiveness from a fellow servant." Or, perhaps you saw yourself to be more like the second servant and imagined what it would be like to be treated so poorly. Few people compare themselves with the bad guy in the parable, but that's exactly what Jesus wants us to do. The point of the parable is to see yourself as the wicked servant. We are the ones who refuse to forgive.

The parables are designed to help us examine our own lives. If you compare yourself to the king, who represents God, you are likely to think you are in pretty good shape. But if you compare yourself to the unmerciful servant, who refused to forgive, you are more likely to see your weaknesses and recognize your need for Jesus.

Remember, in sending his Son Jesus to die for our sins, God has forgiven us an enormous debt. Despite this, we still refuse to forgive others who sin against us. Instead of forgiving, we try to make them pay for their sin by not talking to them or saying unkind things about them or even worse, rejecting their friendship. But God wants us to remember what he did for us, so that in remembering Jesus and his death on the cross we would be more willing to forgive others.

Talk about It

▶ Think of a time when you were forgiven a great debt, or sin against someone else. How did you feel? *(Parents, draw your children out here. Help them to connect with a time when they experienced forgiveness after they had failed or wronged another person. Talk about mercy. Share your own example to encourage them as well. The idea being that we will likely want to extend forgiveness to others when we have experienced forgiveness ourselves.)*

▶ Forgiving others isn't always easy to do. Can you remember a time when it was difficult for you to forgive? *(Not all children will remember a time when it was difficult to forgive. Perhaps you can help them remember a time when a sibling hurt them or their things.)*

▶ What can encourage us in extending forgiveness to others? *(Remembering the following truths can help us in forgiving others who sin against us: All sin is evil and opposed to our loving God. We all have sinned against God. Through Jesus, God has forgiven everyone who believes and places our trust in Jesus, no matter how many times we've sinned. So, if God has forgiven us for the evil things we have done against him, shouldn't we also forgive others?)*

Pray about It

Ask God to help you forgive others when they sin against you.

Going Deeper

The Apostle Paul taught that our motivation for living godly lives should spring from our gratitude for our forgiveness. This is what he taught the Colossians (Colossians 1:9–14). Notice in the Scripture below we are to "walk in a manner worth of the Lord" because "he has delivered us from the domain of darkness and transferred us to the kingdom of his beloved Son, in whom we have redemption, the forgiveness of sins." Granting forgiveness to those who sin against us is one of the fruits, or good works, that flow from a person who is grateful to God.

Colossians 1:9–14 states:

> "And so, from the day we heard, we have not ceased to pray for you, asking that you may be filled with the knowledge of his will in all spiritual wisdom and understanding, so as to walk in a manner worthy of the Lord, fully pleasing to him, bearing fruit in every good work and increasing in the knowledge of God; being strengthened with all power, according to his glorious might, for all endurance and patience with joy; giving thanks to the Father, who has qualified you to share in the inheritance of the saints in light. He has delivered us from the domain of darkness and transferred us to the kingdom of his beloved Son, in whom we have redemption, the forgiveness of sins."

The Parable of the Unmerciful Servant is meant to show us what an incredibly huge debt God has forgiven in removing our sin and that we should treat others the way he has treated us. That doesn't mean it is always easy to forgive; people can do some very unkind things to us. Even so, once we understand how great a debt our sin against God caused for us, and then remember it cost Jesus his life to pay our debt, it will be easier to forgive others. If we refuse to forgive we should beware, for God will not forgive those who refuse to forgive others.

Day Three

Listen Up

Read Luke 7:41–50:

> *"A certain moneylender had two debtors. One owed five hundred denarii, and the other fifty. When they could not*

pay, he cancelled the debt of both. Now which of them will love him more?" Simon answered, "The one, I suppose, for whom he cancelled the larger debt." And he said to him, "You have judged rightly." Then turning toward the woman he said to Simon, "Do you see this woman? I entered your house; you gave me no water for my feet, but she has wet my feet with her tears and wiped them with her hair. You gave me no kiss, but from the time I came in she has not ceased to kiss my feet. You did not anoint my head with oil, but she has anointed my feet with ointment. Therefore I tell you, her sins, which are many, are forgiven—for she loved much. But he who is forgiven little, loves little." And he said to her, "Your sins are forgiven." Then those who were at table with him began to say among themselves, "Who is this, who even forgives sins?" And he said to the woman, "Your faith has saved you; go in peace."

Think about It

A moneylender is a person who helps people when they don't have enough money to buy what they need. If a farmer didn't have enough money to buy seed to plant, he would go to a moneylender to borrow money to purchase seed. Later, when he sold the harvest, he would return the borrowed money to the moneylender, along with an extra amount of money as payment for giving him the loan. We call the extra money paid, interest. Today we call moneylenders, bankers. When we need to borrow money, we go to the bank which is the same thing as a moneylender in Jesus's day.

If a farmer borrowed money from a moneylender and could not repay it because his crops all died, the moneylender could have him thrown into prison. If the moneylender felt sorry for the farmer's trouble, he could forgive the debt. Imagine the joy and relief of the farmer upon hearing such news! Jesus said the bigger the debt that is forgiven, the happier the debtor should be.

Jesus told the Parable of the Moneylender after a woman entered Simon's house and poured a jar full of costly perfume on his feet. Simon, a Pharisee, and the host of the dinner knew the woman's background, that she was a sinner. Jesus, he thought, should know better than to be friendly with a sinful woman. But Jesus saw the woman very differently. Her actions in pouring perfume on his feet showed how thankful she was to Jesus for forgiving her debt of sin. Simon saw the woman as a sinner; Jesus saw her as forgiven and abundantly grateful.

Talk about It

▶ Why did the woman pour perfume on Jesus, kiss his feet, and wipe them with her hair? *(She knew she was a sinner and believed in Jesus and the forgiveness of sin. She was forgiven much, so she loved much.)*

▶ Who are you like in the story? *(Parents, help your children see that we are most like Simon acting as a judge over Jesus and the gospel.)*

▶ Why were the people gathered around the table amazed? *(Parents, if your children can't remember, reread verses 48 and 49 to emphasize why the guests were amazed by the forgiveness of Jesus.)*

Pray about It

Parents, this is perfect opportunity to pray for each of your children, asking God to reveal himself as the only path to forgiveness.

Going Deeper

While the woman's sin appeared greater than Simon's, he did not ask for forgiveness. He didn't even greet Jesus appropriately before dinner. Simon thought he was better than both of them. He looked down at the woman as a sinner and he looked down upon Jesus as a misguided teacher. He placed himself as judge over Jesus. This was a big mistake!

Even though Jesus reclined with Simon for dinner, Simon didn't have a clue who Jesus really was. Simon didn't believe that Jesus was the promised Messiah, sent by God to redeem his people. Simon didn't know Jesus was the Son of God, even though Jesus said God was his Father (Matthew 7:21). He didn't know Jesus came to bring salvation to Israel by taking their sin upon him, even though the prophet Isaiah foretold it (Isaiah 53:5). Simon didn't realize or perhaps he just didn't believe that Jesus held the power to forgive a person's sins, even though Jesus had shown that it was true (Matthew 9:5).

In contrast, th[illegible] she was a sinner. [illegible] sus and the me[illegible] She came runnin[illegible] Jesus forgave her. She is th[illegible] in the parable who owed the larger sum. She was forgiven much, so she loved more.

We don't know if Simon ever turned to Jesus to ask for forgiveness—the Bible doesn't tell that part of the story. He was kind to Jesus. He invited Jesus into his home and gave him food to eat. But still, Simon stood as a judge over Jesus, evaluating him critically. Many people are like Simon. They read the story of Jesus in the Bible and then sit back to judge it rather than run to Jesus for forgiveness like the woman. We are all sinners who need our sins forgiven. While one man's sins may be greater than another, you need only commit one sin, to be called a sinner, and every one of us has sinned. Therefore, we all need to run to Jesus for forgiveness.

Day Four

Listen Up

Read Luke 17:1–4:

> *And he said to his disciples, "Temptations to sin are sure to come, but woe to the one through whom they come! It*

would be better for him if a millstone were hung around his neck and he were cast into the sea than that he should cause one of these little ones to sin. Pay attention to yourselves! If your brother sins, rebuke him, and if he repents, forgive him, and if he sins against you seven times in the day, and turns to you seven times, saying, 'I repent,' you must forgive him."

Think about It

We learned that in addition to parables, Jesus used word pictures and illustrations as he taught. Here Jesus uses the picture of a millstone hung around a person's neck as a grave warning against tempting others to sin. Tempting someone is when you entice them to do something wrong. A millstone is a large flat stone, cut into a circle with a hole in it like a donut. Millstones were used to grind wheat into flour. These stones were so large it took many men to lift one. A millstone could weigh over one thousand pounds. So a person tied to a millstone and cast into the sea would be pulled to the bottom instantly and drowned. Jesus is using this exaggerated illustration to make a point about how terrible it is to tempt another person to sin.

After this dramatic illustration, Jesus repeated his teaching on forgiveness from Luke Chapter 7. Here Jesus tells us we should be willing to keep forgiving people who sin against us even if they do the same thing seven times in a row. Jesus is not asking us to count the number of times a person sins and stop forgiving them once they reach their limit. The point of his teaching is that we should keep on forgiving people no matter how many times they sin. Our motivation for extending forgiveness to others comes from Jesus's continual forgiveness of our sin.

Jesus says, "pay attention to yourselves." Anyone who follows his advice will soon see that we repeat the same sins over and over again. How many times has your mom asked you to be kind to your brother or sister? How many times has she needed to say, "be respectful?" How many times have you gotten angry—more than seven? God doesn't draw a limit on his forgiveness based on how many times we sin against him. Jesus's death on the cross is powerful enough to forgive us a hundred times for the same sin. That doesn't mean we can keep on sinning, but it should help us to forgive others who sin against us.

Talk about It

▶ Jesus said, "pay attention to yourselves." That means we should think about our own lives and where we are most likely to repeat a sin. What sin do you repeat over and over and need God and your parents to keep forgiving you?" *(Parents, draw out your children here by first answering this question yourself. It could be an opportunity to freshly ask your kids' forgiveness for a pattern of anger, impatience, or selfishness.)*

▶ How can looking at our own struggles with sin help us to be more forgiving toward others who repeat sins against us? *(Our sins against God are greater than others sins against us. If we remember that we are sinners too, it can help us be more patient with others who sin against us.)*

▶ Can you think of a time recently when you needed someone to forgive you? *(Parents, help your children think of a recent time they sinned. Then ask them if that was the first time they sinned in that way. It will likely not be the first time—remind them of this the next time someone sins against them, so they too can offer forgiveness.)*

Pray about It

Ask God to help you forgive those who sin against you.

Going Deeper

The Apostle Paul instructed the Galatians to be gentle and humble when we've caught someone else in a sin. Not only are we called to forgive, but we must also remember that we are sinners. After all, the person we forgive today, may be correcting us for our sin tomorrow.

Galatians 6:1–5 says,

> "Brothers, if anyone is caught in any transgression, you who are spiritual should restore him in a spirit of gentleness. Keep watch on yourself, lest you too be tempted. Bear one another's burdens, and so fulfill the law of Christ. For if anyone thinks he is something, when he is nothing, he deceives himself. But let each one test his own work, and then his reason to boast will be in himself alone and not in his neighbor. For each will have to bear his own load."

Those who rebuke others harshly are forgetting just how much we ourselves have been forgiven. Remembering the depth of our own sin against God can help us maintain a humble and gracious posture in addressing others when we catch them sinning against us.

Day Five

Listen Up

Read Luke 17:5–6:

> *The apostles said to the Lord, "Increase our faith!" And the Lord said, "If you had faith like a grain of mustard seed, you could say to this mulberry tree, 'Be uprooted and planted in the sea,' and it would obey you.*

Think about It

Yesterday we heard Jesus tell the disciples they should forgive a person seven times in a row if they continue to sin and seek forgiveness. In our Scripture today, we see how the disciples responded to that teaching. They exclaimed, "Increase our faith!" In other words, they were saying, "You are asking for the impossible. Forgive someone seven times in a row for the very same sin? You have got to be kidding me. If that's true, then you are going to need to give us more faith." Jesus answered them by sharing another word picture, the word picture of The Mustard Seed of Faith.

Now before we look at this popular word picture, we need to remember that it is talking about forgiveness. Sometimes people take this word picture out of context. They use this Scripture and another one like it from Matthew 17 to say whatever they want. They read the passage, that if you have faith you can speak, and a mulberry tree will be uprooted and fly away to the ocean. And then they say, "I guess if you have enough faith you can do anything."

But Jesus is not talking about having enough faith to uproot trees, Jesus is talking about forgiving your brother. He is not saying, if you have faith like a mustard seed you can go around your yard, speak to the plants, and they will uproot and fly into the sea! He is also not saying that if you have the faith like a mustard seed you can do anything.

What Jesus is saying, is that if you have faith in Jesus, and what he did for you on the cross—even a tiny seed of faith in Jesus, you will be able to forgive your brother when he sins against you. The disciples thought they needed a huge amount of faith—but they didn't yet know or fully understand the amazing forgiveness Jesus came to bring.

Today, looking back, we know the full story—that Jesus came to die on the cross to take our punishment. And, if we place our trust in Jesus he will forgive us and welcome us into his heavenly family where we will live with him forever. If we have even a small understanding of how Jesus took all our sins away, we too should be able to forgive a person who repeatedly sins against us out of the joy we have for being forgiven by God.

Talk about It

▶ Did Jesus mean we should all go into our front yard and try to command the bushes to be cast into the sea? *(No, Jesus was only using an exaggerated word picture to teach about forgiveness.)*

▶ How many times are we supposed to forgive someone who keeps sinning in the same ways against us? *(Parents, this is a review question from our Scripture in day one of this week's devotion. Your children are likely going to say "seven times." That's a correct answer from the Bible passage, but help them to see what the "seven times" represents— that we should continue forgiving others.)*

▶ Jesus said we are supposed to have faith. What are we supposed to have faith in? *(Jesus is the object of our faith. Faith is the belief that something is true. Our faith rests in Jesus, that he really did die on the cross for our sin and rise again so that we too will one day rise and spend eternity with him. If we believe that is true—if we have faith that we have been forgiven, that opens our hearts to forgiving others. Because we follow Jesus and have his Spirit, we can treat others the same way he treats us.)*

Pray about It

Ask Jesus to help you remember what he did on the cross for you, so that you can find strength to forgive those who sin against you.

Going Deeper

The forgiveness of our sin should lead us to worship God. The popular traditional hymn, "Glory, Glory, Hallelujah" began as a Spiritual and folks have since added verses to express the transforming power of forgiveness. Consider these lyrics:

Glory, glory, hallelujah!
Since I laid my burdens down.
Glory, glory, hallelujah!
Since I laid my burdens down!
Friends don't treat me like they used to
Since I laid my burdens down.
Friends don't treat me like they used to
Since I laid my burdens down!
I'm goin' home to be with Jesus
Since I laid my burdens down.
I'm goin' home to be with Jesus
Since I laid my burdens down!
I won't treat you like I used to
Since I laid my burdens down.
I won't treat you like I used to
Since I laid my burdens down!

Before we laid our burdens down (confessed our sin and asked Jesus to save us), we held grudges, became bitter, gossiped against those who sinned against us, and treated them unkindly. But now, having been forgiven by Christ and welcomed into his family, we should treat people differently. Now we can extend the same forgiveness Jesus extends to us. The result is that we multiply their joy and motivate them to sing, "Friends don't treat me like they used to since I laid my burdens down."

Week 6

Who Is My Neighbor?

Let's Look at the Week. . .

This week we are going to study the Parable of the Good Samaritan and look to answer the question: "Who is my neighbor?" Back in Jesus's day, the Samaritans were a group of people who were hated by the Jews. The bad feelings between the Jews and the Samaritans began hundreds of years earlier, around the time when the ten northern tribes of Israel were taken captive, and the men of Israel brought back to Babylon. The prisoners included Jews who lived in the land of Samaria. After the war was over, the King of Assyria resettled their city with idol worshippers from foreign cities like Babylon. Shortly after they resettled the land, God sent lions against those who were worshipping idols instead of the one, true God of Israel.

In an effort to honor the God of Israel and thwart further lion attacks, the King of Assyria sent a priest of Israel to Samaria to teach the foreigners how to worship the one, true God of Israel (2 Kings 24:28). But instead of worshipping the one, true God of Israel, the foreigners in Samaria blended the two religions and maintained their idol worship. In addition, they married the Israelite women of the land and led them to do the same wicked things. Seventy year later, when the captive Jews in Babylon finally returned home from exile, they discovered the mixed worship in Samaria and despised the Samaritans (people of Samaria) for their idolatry.

By the time Jesus began his ministry, a deep hatred had developed between the Jews and the Samaritans. Israel's hatred for the Samaritans made it difficult for them to accept Jesus's teaching and the idea that God wanted to save both Jew and Gentile. They forgot the promise God gave Abraham to bless all the nations of the earth through him (Genesis 22:18). Because Jesus came to bring salvation to people from every tribe and nation, he treated the Samaritans very differently.

Get Ready

The action word of the week is love.

Love is a feeling of deep, lasting affection. Think of the joy you feel when your mom or dad give you a big hug. One the best examples of love is when a man and woman fall in love, decide to get married, and promise to spend the rest of their lives together as a couple.

There is a problem with the word *love*; we use it all the time instead of the word *like*. We say we love milkshakes, a sunny day at the beach, popcorn, chocolate, rainbows, hot cars, the smell of cinnamon, and a ton of other things. But, when we say we love something like pizza, we don't mean we want to spend the rest of our lives with pizza, like we do when we talk about love in marriage. When we say we love football, we don't mean we will only love football and never love another sport as long as we shall live.

This week we will learn that we are supposed to love God and love our neighbor (other people around us). You'll see that love is something that's much easier for us to say than it is to put into practice.

Who Is My Neighbor?

(This activity will encourage your children to consider their neighbors.)

Supplies:

- Ingredients for chocolate chip cookies
- Gift bags or containers

How well do you know your neighbors? Imagine your house is the center of a tic-tac-toe grid. Can you name the eight neighbors closest to you? They are the people whose apartments or property sit directly across or diagonal from your house in all directions. Draw a tick-tack-toe grid and fill in their names and family members. Most folks can name at least one neighbor, but few people know the names of all eight.

Bake a batch of cookies and split it in half. Give half to the neighbor you know the best and then take the second half to the neighbor you know the least. Go as a family, knock on their door when they are home, and say something like: We live next to you and haven't gotten a chance to get to know you so we thought we would drop off a bag of cookies and introduce ourselves.

Now if you are feeling a bit uncomfortable with the whole idea, relax, that's normal. It is often difficult to step out of our comfort zone. Keep that in mind when you study the Parable of the Good Samaritan this week.

Day One

Listen Up

Read Luke 10:21–24:

> *In that same hour he rejoiced in the Holy Spirit and said, "I thank you, Father, Lord of heaven and earth, that you have hidden these things from the wise and understanding and revealed them to little children; yes, Father, for such was your gracious will. All things have been handed over to me by my Father, and no one knows who the Son is except the Father, or who the Father is except the Son and anyone to whom the Son chooses to reveal him."*
>
> *Then turning to the disciples he said privately, "Blessed are the eyes that see what you see! For I tell you that many prophets and kings desired to see what you see, and did not see it, and to hear what you hear, and did not hear it."*

Think about It

When Jesus said God the Father helped the little children understand his teaching, he wasn't saying that only kids understand the parables. Jesus was talking about all God's children who make up the family of God. (That's why he describes God as a Father to them.) When we turn from our sin and believe in Jesus, we too are welcomed into the family of God—whether we are seven years old or sixty. When Jesus said the meaning of the parables hidden from the wise, he was talking about the people who rejected Jesus—those who thought they were wise—so wise that they thought they didn't need Jesus. Sinful pride has a way of blinding us to the important truth we need to know.

Did you ever tell someone "I don't need help. I can do it myself," only to fail and then realize you were wrong—you really did need help? The religious rulers in Jesus day and the Jews who listened to them, made fun of Jesus. They didn't think they needed his help or his teaching. But God the Father drew others into his family by opening their eyes to see their need for Jesus.

The disciples didn't realize how fortunate they were to live during the time of Jesus. For hundreds of years the kings and prophets of Israel who loved God longed to see God deliver his people from the curse of sin. But they died before Jesus ever came. Jesus wanted the disciples to understand how blessed they were to walk with him.

We too are blessed like the disciples because we get to read in the Bible what Jesus told the disciples privately. Reading the Bible is like learning directly from Jesus! But even with it all explained to us, we need the Holy Spirit to open our eyes and hearts to help us believe. Many people read these same Bible passages and walk away without believing in Jesus and his teachings.

Talk about It

▶ Why did Jesus say the disciples were blessed? *(Jesus said the disciples were blessed because they got to see him and hear his teaching, the teaching many prophets and kings longed to hear.)*

▶ Why are we blessed like the disciples? *(We are blessed like the disciples because we have the life and teaching of Jesus recorded in the Bible for us to read and believe. We get the same inside look at Jesus the disciples did.)*

▶ Why doesn't everyone who reads the Bible believe in Jesus? *(Just as in Jesus's day, God, by his Spirit, must open our eyes before we will turn from sin and trust in Jesus. Otherwise, we will naturally choose to live our lives apart from him.)*

Pray about It

Pray for God to open your eyes and heart so that you and all your family will turn from their sin and put their faith in Jesus.

Going Deeper

To better understand the Parable of the Good Samaritan, it is important to look at the verses that come before it. At the beginning of the tenth chapter of Luke's gospel, we see that Jesus sent out seventy-two disciples into the towns and gave them the power to cast out demons and heal the people just as he did. When the disciples returned, they excitedly reported their success. They too could command the demons to leave the people they possessed!

Our Scripture today is the prayer of thanksgiving Jesus prayed when he heard their report. Jesus explained that of all the people in the world that ever lived, the disciples were blessed to see the Messiah, God's promised deliverer. Many of the prophets and kings of the Old Testament longed to see him and hear his teaching but died before they ever had the chance.

There is also something very interesting hidden in Jesus's prayer. Jesus said that we need him to open our eyes before we can see who he really is. That's because Satan has "blinded the minds of unbelievers, to keep them from seeing the light of the gospel" (2 Corinthians 4:4). Jesus didn't give that information to everyone. Notice Jesus turned to the disciples privately (Luke 10:23) to tell them. Jesus also spoke in hard to understand parables to hide the truth from the mockers and unbelievers, but he explained the parables to his disciples. To those whom God called, he gave grace and a curiosity to learn. The parables drew them into a relationship with God. Once again we see Jesus sharing how fortunate the disciples were to be given the knowledge to decode the secret hidden messages of the parables.

Day Two

Listen Up

Read Luke 10:25–29:

> *And behold, a lawyer stood up to put him to the test, saying, "Teacher, what shall I do to inherit eternal life?" He said to him, "What is written in the Law? How do you read it?" And he answered, "You shall love the Lord your God with all your heart and with all your soul and with all your strength and with all your mind, and your*

neighbor as yourself." And he said to him, "You have answered correctly; do this, and you will live."

But he, desiring to justify himself, said to Jesus, "And who is my neighbor?"

Think about It

The lawyer from our passage today is a Jewish religious leader, not a Roman attorney. His question is designed to test Jesus. But the tables turn quickly on the man when Jesus asks him to answer his own question. Now Jesus is in control. In seconds, Jesus is out of the trap and has the man providing his own answer.

Although the lawyer provided the correct answer, he wasn't satisfied. He believed that he had loved God with all his heart, but he wasn't sure about the second part of the command that talked about loving his neighbor. To feel good about himself for obeying the command, the lawyer wanted to know who he was supposed to love as a neighbor. This also means he wanted to know who he did not have to love. The lawyer was looking to make his circle of neighbors as small as possible. The smaller the number of neighbors, the better chance he could prove he had loved them.

So, what about us? Who do we consider our neighbors? Most people today limit their neighbors to the three or four families who live closest to them. If you live out in the countryside, you might only have one other home close to you. Does that mean you only have one family to love? If you live in the city and have twenty families that live the same distance away, does that mean you must love all twenty families?

Jesus wasn't trying to set guidelines that tell us who we have to love. Jesus was interested in the man's heart. Jesus knew that the lawyer wanted to minimize his circle of people to love. Tomorrow we will witness the man's great surprise in listening to the Parable of the Good Samaritan.

Talk about It

▶ The Bible verse says the man wanted to justify himself. What do you think that means? *(Justify is a legal term meaning to declare innocent. The man wanted to prove that he was innocent—that he was righteous and had obeyed the Law.)*

▶ Can anyone love God with all their heart, soul, and strength? *(No, we all fall short of loving God with all our heart, soul, and strength. None of us can keep God's commands perfectly and we all love the things of the world more than God.)*

▶ How have you done with loving God with all your heart, soul, and strength? *(Parents, take initiative to answer this one first yourself. Then draw out your children and help them to see the man in the story as blind to his own sin. He moved on quickly to ask, "Who is my neighbor?" when he should have realized he loved himself more than he loved God.)*

Pray about It

Ask God to help you love him with all your heart, soul, and strength.

Going Deeper

The Jews did not believe that Gentiles (non-Jews) were their neighbors. In fact, the Jews believed it was wrong to treat Gentiles as neighbors, unless they fully embraced the Jewish faith and turned from their pagan ways. Consider how God instructed Israel when sending them in to conquer the land:

> "But in the cities of these peoples that the LORD your God is giving you for an inheritance, you shall save alive nothing that breathes, but you shall devote them to complete destruction, the Hittites and the Amorites, the Canaanites and the Perizzites, the Hivites and the Jebusites, as the LORD your God has commanded, that they may not teach you to do according to all their abominable practices that they have done for their gods, and so you sin against the LORD your God" (Deuteronomy 20:16–18).

In addition to seeing Gentiles as outsiders, the Israelites rejected any Jews who were judged and found guilty for committing serious sins and forced out of the city. They were also labeled as outsiders and not treated as neighbors. Then, if you allow yourself, as the lawyers did, to start judging who does and who does not love God, you can exclude any number of people from the circle of "neighbor." In the end, many of the Jews only considered the people they knew well, who came from their own tribe or even their own family, as a neighbor.

Listen Up

Read Luke 10:30–35:

> *Jesus replied, "A man was going down from Jerusalem to Jericho, and he fell among robbers, who stripped him and beat him and departed, leaving him half dead. Now by chance a priest was going down that road, and when he saw him he passed by on the other side. So likewise a Levite, when he came to the place and saw him, passed by on the other side. But a Samaritan, as he journeyed, came to where he was, and when he saw him, he had compassion. He went to him and bound up his wounds, pouring on oil and wine. Then he set him on his own animal and brought him to an inn and took care of him. And the next day he took out two denarii and gave them to the innkeeper, saying, 'Take care of him, and whatever more you spend, I will repay you when I come back.'*

The route from Jerusalem to Jericho is well known for its dangers. The 18-mile downhill journey drops 1,700 feet, placing Jericho a half mile lower than the city of Jerusalem. Much of the journey is through a barren wasteland where there is no water along the way. No one lives along the road, so only fellow travelers are available to help if a snake bites your leg or a scorpion stings you. Large boulders, rock outcroppings and caves fill the ravine, providing thousands of hideouts for thieves. Should a robber strike, your cries for help would echo through the ravines, and no one would know exactly where you were.

Think about It

In response to the lawyer's question, "Who is my neighbor?" Jesus told the Parable of the Good Samaritan. It is the story of a man attacked by robbers on the dangerous downhill journey from Jerusalem to Jericho. Three men came upon the injured man. The first two men, a Priest, and a Levite, served in the temple; the priests offered the sacrifices while the Levites served alongside the priests. Neither of these two important men of Israel stopped to help the injured man. At this point in the story we are left with a question—who will help this man?

Jesus is setting the lawyer up for a twist. The lawyer is likely expecting another Jew to help the man, perhaps a family member, who the Law allowed to care for the injured man. But instead, Jesus brought a despised Samaritan into the story to help the injured traveler. The Samaritan didn't just call for help; he touched the dying man and carried him away. Giving of his time and money, the Samaritan risked his reputation, knowing he could be criticized for helping a Jew. He took the extraordinary step taking the man to a place where he could receive proper care. The Samaritan treated the Jew like a neighbor—this twist in Jesus's story would have shocked the lawyer for sure. If he had to consider a Samaritan his neighbor, then his circle of neighbors was huge; it could include anyone! And that was Jesus's point—we need to be ready to love anyone God places in our path and treat everyone with kindness like a neighbor.

Think about your life. When someone is teasing another child in your class, do you come to their rescue? That is treating them like your neighbor. When a new family moves into your neighborhood, do you welcome their children into your circle of friends? That's treating them like your neighbor. When you welcome your younger brother or sister to join you for a walk—that's treating them like a neighbor.

Talk about It

▶ Who demonstrated love in this parable? *(The Samaritan demonstrated love by stopping to help the injured man.)*

▶ Why didn't the priest or the Levite stop to help the man? *(If the man was dead or died in their attempt to help him, the priest or the Levite would have become ceremonially unclean and unable to serve in the temple for days.)*

▶ How did Jesus surprise the religious lawyer? *(Jesus made the third man in his parable a Samaritan, whom the Jews hated. Having the Samaritan help the injured Jew made the priest and Levite look bad for not helping.)*

▶ How might you respond if you were taking a walk and encountered a man, beaten on the side of the road? What if the man was dirty and destitute? *(Parents, draw out your children here so they connect with the story. Help them recognize that the response of the Jews and Samaritans might not be too far off from our response if we were in the same situation.)*

Pray about It

Ask God to help you show compassion to people in need.

Going Deeper

While the actions of the priest and Levite may seem very unkind, both men had been taught the Law since they were young kids. They likely remembered what they were taught about the Law; that if they touched a dead body they became unclean and therefore unable to serve in the temple. While we know from the story that the man on the side of the road was not yet dead, he was in bad shape. He might have looked dead, or even if he was still moving the priest and the Levite would have concluded that he could die at any moment. The law of Moses was clear on that point, "No one shall make himself unclean for the dead among his people, except for his closest relatives" (Leviticus 21:1–2).

Day Four

Listen Up

Read Luke 10:36–37:

> *Which of these three, do you think, proved to be a neighbor to the man who fell among the robbers?" He said, "The one who showed him mercy." And Jesus said to him, "You go, and do likewise."*

Think about It

Remember the question the lawyer asked Jesus—"Who is my neighbor?" Jesus forced the lawyer to answer his own question. The lawyer, wanting to justify himself (felt like he lived a good life and obeyed God), was looking to minimize his circle of people he had to love. He created a short mental list—his wife and children, father and mother, other family members who lived close by, and perhaps a few Jews that lived immediately to the left and right of his home.

Jesus used the parable to challenge the lawyer's thinking. His charge to the lawyer, "You go, and do likewise," means that the lawyer must enlarge his circle to include the Samaritans. That was unthinkable.

Imagine you are having a birthday party and your mom asks you to invite three kids that you dislike—wouldn't that sound crazy to you? That's kind of what Jesus is teaching—that we even need to show love to those who we dislike and treat them with kindness.

The lawyer believed he needed to obey the Law to be accepted by God and thought if a person tried hard enough, he could obey the Law. But the truth is that it is impossible to obey God's Law perfectly. There is only one person who obeyed God's Law perfectly—Jesus. Jesus loved everyone as a neighbor. He never turned anyone away, but welcomed all to come and he would give them rest (Matthew 11:28).

Talk about It

▶ What do you think the lawyer thought about as he walked away from Jesus? *(Parents, there is no perfect answer here. Draw out your children. He may have thought Jesus was crazy for suggesting he love the Samaritans, or we might find one day that God touched him through the story and he repented. But one thing is certain, the lawyer never expected Jesus to answer his question, "Who is my neighbor?" with the answer—even the Samaritans!)*

▶ We all have people in our lives that are difficult to love for one reason or another. Who is hardest for you to love? Who is your Samaritan? *(Parents, help your children to identify a person that's difficult to love. Then, encourage them to connect their situation to the parable. That person they are identifying is their neighbor. Take time to first tell them about a person whom you find difficult to love.)*

▶ What does it mean to love someone like you love yourself? *(Help your children see how carefully we cater to ourselves, then help them to see how we need to use that same thinking in reaching out to others.)*

Pray about It

Ask God for the grace to love our Samaritans, those people we find it difficult to love.

Going Deeper

When the lawyer first approached Jesus, he thought that he was good enough to go to heaven. But if he was required to love the Samaritans, heaven was out of reach. Jesus wanted him to see that none of us can get to heaven by doing good works. The religious rulers of Israel made the circle of people they needed to love small. That allowed them to say they obeyed the Law to love their neighbor. But if Jesus was correct, and the Samaritans were their neighbors too, then no one could obey the Law, which means it is impossible to get to heaven by your own works.

The truth is that none of us are good enough, righteous enough, or can fulfill all the Law to qualify for heaven (Romans 3:10–12). Only Jesus lived a perfect life and fulfilled God's Law. He died to take our sin and now offers his perfect record of love, in exchange for our sin. The only way we get to heaven is by trusting in Jesus.

Day Five

Listen Up

Read John 4:7–14:

> *A woman from Samaria came to draw water. Jesus said to her, "Give me a drink" (For his disciples had gone away into the city to buy food.) The Samaritan woman said to him, "How is it that you, a Jew, ask for a drink from me, a woman of Samaria?" (For Jews have no dealings with Samaritans.) Jesus answered her, "If you knew the gift of God, and who it is that is saying to you, 'Give me a drink,' you would have asked him, and he would have given you living water." The woman said to him, "Sir, you have nothing to draw water with, and the well is deep. Where do you get that living water? Are you greater than our father Jacob? He gave us the well and drank from it himself, as did his sons and his livestock." Jesus said to her, "Everyone who drinks of this water will be thirsty again, but whoever drinks of the water that I will give him will never be thirsty again. The water that I will give him will become in him a spring of water welling up to eternal life."*

Think about It

Like the Samaritan traveler who stopped to help the robbery victim, Jesus reached out to encourage a Samaritan woman. Jesus, a Jew, treated the Samaritan as his neighbor. He spoke with her, even though that could make him look bad. It was considered inappropriate (not the right thing to do) for a man to speak as Jesus did to a woman, especially in public. On top of that, Jesus asked her to give him a drink. Taking a drink from a Samaritan would have made Jesus ceremonially unclean—the same concern the priest and Levite confronted in helping the badly injured man they found along the roadside.

While the woman was not a victim of a robbery, she was a victim of the curse and a sinner in need of help. Like the beaten man on the side of the road, she needed someone to rescue her—and Jesus came as a neighbor. Jesus offered the woman salvation using the word pictures of living water and an everlasting spring. Then Jesus told the woman straight up that he was the Messiah. Jesus's words transformed the woman's life. After her conversation at the well, she spread the news about Jesus in the village, and many came to Jesus because of her testimony. Read the rest of the story to see what happened in John 4:27–30.

It seems clear from the story that the Samaritan woman became a Christian that day. Believers in Jesus will one day meet her in heaven and hear more of this true story. Remember the Parable of the Good Samaritan? If Jesus acted like the priest or Levite from that story, he would have ignored the woman, and found a way to obtain his own drink, leaving the woman lost in her sin. Aren't you glad Jesus is not afraid to love a sinner like me and you?

Talk about It

▸ How is the story of Jesus meeting the woman at the well like the Parable of the Good Samaritan? *(Both stories involve a Samaritan and a Jew and speak of individuals who were willing to love their neighbor, even when it conflicted with what the culture or the Law.)*

▸ How are we like the Samaritan woman? *(We are all sinners in need of the Holy Spirit [living water].)*

▸ Who is the Samaritan in your life that God wants you to love? *(Parents, think of a person in your own life who is difficult to love. Then draw out your children to see if there is someone they can reach out to love.)*

Pray about It

Ask for God's help to love and reach out to others in love.

Going Deeper

Jesus loved his neighbor perfectly. Consider some of these examples:

Jesus touched a dead body even though by doing so he would be ceremonially unclean. He didn't shy away from considering the dead man his neighbor. "And when the Lord saw her, he had compassion on her and said to her, 'Do not weep.' Then he came up and touched the bier, and the bearers stood still. And he said, 'Young man, I say to you, arise.' And the dead man sat up and began to speak, and Jesus gave him to his mother" (Luke 7:13–15).

According to the Law, those with leprosy were cast outside the camp and identified as unclean. Over time, the Jews even rejected their own family members with the disease. But Jesus treated the lepers as his neighbor. "When he came down from the mountain, great crowds followed him. And behold, a leper came to him and knelt before him, saying, 'Lord, if you will, you can make me clean.' And Jesus stretched out his hand and touched him, saying, 'I will; be clean.' And immediately his leprosy was cleansed" (Matthew 8:1–3).

Another group of people the Jews rejected were the tax collectors. But once again, Jesus reached out to them as seen in Mark 2:15–17:

> "And as he reclined at table in his house, many tax collectors and sinners were reclining with Jesus and his disciples, for there were many who followed him. And the scribes of the Pharisees, when they saw that he was eating with sinners and tax collectors, said to his disciples, 'Why does he eat with tax collectors and sinners?' And when Jesus heard it, he said to them, 'Those who are well have no need of a physician, but those who are sick. I came not to call the righteous, but sinners.'"

Week 7

Teach Me to Pray

Let's Look at the Week. . .

This week we are going to study the topic of prayer. Prayer is simply talking to God. Luke tells us that Jesus often withdrew from the crowds and went alone to desolate places to pray (Luke 5:16). With people pressing in for hours on end to ask Jesus to heal them, it is understandable that Jesus grew tired and needed a break. But he didn't pull away to enjoy a personal vacation with his disciples. He left the noise and demands of the crowd to get alone so that he could talk to his Father in heaven.

The disciples saw how seriously Jesus took prayer. Jesus pulled away to pray quite often, and his example stirred a desire in the disciples to pray—but they were not sure how to go about it. So, one day they asked him to teach them. The prayer Jesus taught the disciples to get them started is preserved in the Bible for us today. People call it "the Lord's Prayer." This week we will study the Lord's Prayer along with the parable Jesus taught as part of his instruction to the disciples.

Get Ready

The action word of the week is pray.

Praying is talking to God. When we talk to our brother or sister, our friends, or parents, it is easy because they are standing right in front of us. Even when we call our friends on the phone, we hear their voices. When we ask someone on the phone, "How are you doing?" we expect them to reply by saying "I'm fine" or "I'm not well."

The challenge with praying is it can feel awkward. We can't see God standing in front of us and he doesn't reply to the things we say. That can leave us wondering if God really does hear us. It can also leave us unsure of what God is saying back to us. The disciples saw Jesus praying but were not sure how to pray themselves so they asked Jesus to teach them.

This week we will learn how Jesus taught them how to pray. We will also study the parables Jesus used to encourage them in prayer.

We Talk a Lot

(This activity encourages us in our relationship and communication with God.)

Prayer is simply talking to God. If we believe God is our Father, we should talk to him. We do that in our prayers. To demonstrate just how much children and parents communicate, try to go two hours without any conversation between you and your children. (Plan the start of this exercise around a common activity where you are all together such as during a meal.) Mom and Dad can talk to one another and the children can talk between themselves but try to continue your normal interactions without communicating parent to child.

Of course everyone should talk if an emergency pops up, but other than that, see if you can go on with your life for two hours without conversation.

When the two hours are up, discuss how it felt to remain quiet and not communicate. Parents and children talk to each other all the time. Children ask their parents for things that they need, like something to eat or a ride to a friend's house. Parents, remind their children to do their chores. Both parents and children express their love for one another through words. While we can't see God in the same way as our other family members, God is no less real and wants us to talk with him every day. He loves us and wants us to enjoy a relationship with him, just as we do our earthly parents.

Day One

Listen Up

Read Luke 11:1–4:

> *Now Jesus was praying in a certain place, and when he finished, one of his disciples said to him, "Lord, teach us to pray, as John taught his disciples." And he said to them,*

"When you pray, say: Father, hallowed be your name. Your kingdom come. Give us each day our daily bread, and forgive us our sins, for we ourselves forgive everyone who is indebted to us. And lead us not into temptation."

Think about It

Prayer is talking to God but that can be confusing. After all, you are talking to someone you can't see. Aren't you glad the disciples asked Jesus to teach them how to pray, and that his answer is recorded in the Bible for us? Jesus's answer to the disciples teaches us about prayer. Perhaps the most important lesson is that prayer is not long or complicated. Notice how short Jesus's prayer is. As we said in the introduction, prayer is simply talking to God and Jesus gives us four guidelines that we can use as we pray.

First, we can praise God in our prayers. Praise is telling God that he is wonderful. We can praise the name of God and pray his rule over the entire world (his kingdom). Second, it is OK to ask God to provide our basic needs (our daily bread). God knows that we need food to eat, clothes to wear, a place to live, and water to drink, and he wants us to ask him to provide.

The third guideline deals with our greatest problem—sin. We need God to forgive us for the sins we commit, and we need God's help to forgive those who sin against us. Jesus said we should share these needs with God in our prayers. The fourth guideline is also about sin. We should pray for help regarding temptation and our ability to fight our future battle against sin. We need God's help to win that fight.

Now these are not the only things you should pray for. You can talk to God about anything. But if you ever get stuck, and don't know what to pray, simply go back to the Lord's Prayer and pray through each of these four items.

Talk about It

▶ Why do people call this passage, the Lord's Prayer? *(The passage is called the Lord's Prayer because he is the one who wrote it.)*

▶ Can you remember something Jesus taught us to pray in the Lord's Prayer? *(Parents, use this as an opportunity to review the four guidelines from the Lord's Prayer. See if your children can remember them all.)*

▶ Can you give an example of something you could pray for that fits one of the guidelines Jesus gave us? *(This is where you want to help your children apply the Scripture. Have them think of a sin they could confess and ask forgiveness for, someone they need help to forgive, or perhaps they could ask God for a daily need like food or clothing. Try and make the prayer specific. Rather than ask for daily bread, pray that God will help their parents do well at work and in providing for the needs of the family.)*

Pray about It

Take time to pray through the Lord's Prayer covering each of the four guidelines mentioned in the discussion.

Going Deeper

When you study the parables of Jesus, the context helps you understand what the parable is trying to teach and how to apply it to your life. Tomorrow we will look at the Parable of the Friend Arriving at Midnight. Although prayer is not mentioned in this parable, Jesus shared it in response to the disciples' desire to learn to pray. Jesus told the parable in response to the question of the disciples to "teach us to pray." In order to understand why Jesus taught this parable, we need to look back at the context, or the verses surrounding the passage. In those verses, we see Jesus teaching the disciples to pray the Lord's Prayer.

The Lord's Prayer is found in two of the four gospel accounts. We'll take a closer look at the longer version Matthew presents in his gospel later in the week.

Day Two

Listen Up

Read Luke 11:5–10:

> *And he said to them, "Which of you who has a friend will go to him at midnight and say to him, 'Friend, lend me three loaves, for a friend of mine has arrived on a journey, and I have nothing to set before him'; and he will answer from within, 'Do not bother me; the door is now shut, and my children are with me in bed. I cannot get up and give you anything'? I tell you, though he will not get up and give him anything because he is his friend, yet because of his impudence he will rise and give him whatever he needs. "And I tell you, ask, and it will be given to you; seek, and you will find; knock, and it will be opened to you. For everyone who asks receives, and the one who seeks finds, and to the one who knocks it will be opened.*

Think about It

By reading the verses that come before our parable, the passage we discussed yesterday, it is easy to see that the Parable of the Friend Arriving at Midnight is meant to teach us something about prayer. Jesus used this parable to instruct the disciples on how to pray.

Now most homes in Jerusalem consisted of one small room. When bedtime arrived, everyone slept on the main floor of that one large room. Once the lamps were turned off, and everyone was asleep, it was not so easy to get up and walk to the door without stepping on someone.

When the neighbor came knocking, asking for bread, the man of the house did not want to get up, step around his family in the dark, and try and find bread for his friend. But rather than roll over and go back to sleep, he did get up. He probably thought, "Since I'm already wake, I better answer the door. Then I can go back to sleep." So the owner of the house got up and gave him the bread, not because he was a friend, but because of his impudence (rudeness).

So what is Jesus trying to teach? Is God actually sleeping and bothered by our requests? No, God is just the opposite. He is glad to help us. This parable is a story that points to a greater truth or reality. If a man who is asleep at night is willing to give a neighbor bread to get rid of him, how much more will God, who is all patient, loving, and kind give us what we need when we ask? God loves to answer the prayers of his children.

After telling them the parable, Jesus encouraged the disciples to pray using the same imagery in the parable. Jesus said, "knock, and it will be opened to you." Clearly, God is eager to answer our prayers. If we knock on God's door through our prayers, God will open it for us, and give us what we need. Now some folks take this promise too far. They say that if we ask for anything by faith, God will give it to us. But they forget that God is a loving Father, and he is not going to give us something that will harm us. So we don't always get what we ask for, but we always get what we truly need.

Talk about It

▶ What is Jesus trying to teach his disciples through this parable? *(Jesus wants the disciples to know that God is willing to answer their prayers.)*

▶ Can you think of a time when God answered one of your prayers? *(Parents, help your children remember a time when God answered one of their prayers or share a time when God answered one of your prayers.)*

▶ Think back to the Lord's Prayer as a guide. What are one or two things you could ask God for in prayer? *(Parents, the Lord's Prayer is a helpful guide. For instance, it teaches us to ask for daily bread, which represents the basic needs of life. Steer your children in that direction rather than praying for recreational extras like a bigger bike, a vacation to Disney, or a million dollars.)*

Pray about It

Pray the prayers you discussed in answering the last question.

Going Deeper

In Jesus's day, hospitality was an important value. When someone came to visit after a long journey, the host was obligated to provide the guest with something to eat and drink. However, when an unexpected guest showed up at midnight, the man had no bread to offer him. In those days, people didn't have their own oven. Communities shared a stone or brick oven and took turns using it to bake bread. Perhaps the host remembered which neighbor turn it was to bake bread earlier that day. Even though it was late, the he still approached his neighbor's door and knocked, and asked for help.

Day Three

Listen Up

Read Luke 11:11–13:

> *What father among you, if his son asks for a fish, will instead of a fish give him a serpent; or if he asks for an egg, will give him a scorpion? If you then, who are evil, know how to give good gifts to your children, how much more will the heavenly Father give the Holy Spirit to those who ask him!"*

The two most poisonous of all Israel's scorpions are the Israeli yellow scorpion (known as the deathstalker) and the black fat-tailed scorpion (known as the southern man-killer). The sting from either one of these scorpions is so potent it can kill a fully-grown man.

The venom of a scorpion is found in a sharp pointy barb in the tip of its tail. A thrust of the barb into its victim's flesh, causes the venom to release. Some people think that yellow scorpions are more poisonous than black scorpions but that's not true. The biggest danger from a scorpion sting is the effect of the poison on the brain (which can make a person unconscious) and upon the heart (which causes severe heart failure and even death). So, no father would ever give his child a scorpion.

Think about It

To further encourage the faith and prayer life of the disciples, Jesus gave them a second encouragement. Jesus used the example of a son asking his father for something to eat. But to make a point, Jesus gave a few exaggerated responses to the son's request—a serpent instead of a fish and a scorpion instead of an egg. Imagine you are out working in the lawn with your dad. After a few hours of work you start to get hungry, so you ask your dad if you can break for lunch. Your dad tosses you a sealed cloth bag and says, "Eat this."

As soon as the sack hits the ground, the bag starts to move and you recognize the identifiable vibration of a rattlesnake. If that really happened, you would think your dad was crazy because no father would ever give his son a live poisonous snake to eat for lunch. In this case, the craziness of the story helps us remember the lesson Jesus taught.

After sharing the exaggerated word picture, Jesus made his point. If earthly fathers (who we know are sinners and are not perfect, and can get angry) give their children good gifts, how much more should we expect God (who has no sin and is only good) will also give us good gifts. Just like in the Lord's Prayer, this parable teaches us that God is our Father who is poised and ready to give us good things, not bad things. The best gift of all is the Holy Spirit. When we turn away from our sin and place our trust in Jesus, he places his Holy Spirit into our hearts as our helper. How amazing—the Spirit of God lives inside us! That's the best gift we could ever receive.

So, what we learn from Jesus's teaching in the two parables is that God our Father is very willing to answer our prayers and ready to give us the best gift of all—the Holy Spirit. Knowing that, we should be quick to pray to God and ask for his help when we are in need.

Talk about It

▶ Why did Jesus use the example of a scorpion? *(Jesus used an exaggerated example to make a point. Everyone would agree that a dad would never give those things to his children, even if he was a bit on the mean side.)*

▶ What was Jesus trying to teach through these exaggerated examples? *(Jesus explains—if an earthly dad knows how to give his children good things, how much more should we expect God in heaven to give us good things.)*

▶ How can remembering God is our Father encourage us to pray, believing he will answer? *(Fathers love to give good things to their children. If we think of God as a ruler who has millions of servants and we are merely one of many, we might think God would never answer our prayers. But if we know that God is our Father in heaven, and we are his children, then we can expect he would want to hear about and provide for our needs.)*

Pray about It

Take time to pray and ask God for his help with something. Feel free to repeat yesterday's prayer if you would like.

Going Deeper

Jesus often repeated his teaching and when he did, he didn't always say the exact same things. Notice the differences in the way Matthew recorded Jesus's teaching of a similar lesson:

> "Ask, and it will be given to you; seek, and you will find; knock, and it will be opened to you. For everyone who asks receives, and the one who seeks finds, and to the one who knocks it will be opened. Or which one of you, if his son asks him for bread, will give him a stone? Or if he asks for a fish, will give him a serpent? If you then, who are evil, know how to give good gifts to your children, how much more will your Father who is in heaven give good things to those who ask him!" (Matthew 7:7–11).

Jesus taught the above lesson as part of the Sermon on the Mount. That was most likely a different occasion than the one Luke recorded where Jesus taught the Lord's Prayer. Here, Jesus spoke of a stone instead of scorpion and didn't mention the Holy Spirit. It can be helpful to point out parallel passages to your children and let them know Jesus taught the same thing multiple times in different settings. It is not like Matthew or Luke remembered wrong—was it a rock or scorpion? Jesus taught the same lesson with two different illustrations to two different groups of people.

Listen Up

Read Luke 18:1–8:

> *And he told them a parable to the effect that they ought always to pray and not lose heart. He said, "In a certain city there was a judge who neither feared God nor respected man. And there was a widow in that city who kept coming to him and saying, 'Give me justice against my adversary.' For a while he refused, but afterward he said to himself, 'Though I neither fear God nor respect man, yet because this widow keeps bothering me, I will give her justice, so that she will not beat me down by her continual coming.'" And the Lord said, "Hear what the unrighteous judge says. And will not God give justice to his elect, who cry to him day and night? Will he delay long over them? I tell you, he will give justice to them speedily. Nevertheless, when the Son of Man comes, will he find faith on earth?"*

Think about It

The Parable of the Unrighteous Judge uses a "lesser" situation to teach a "greater" truth. The lesser is the unrighteous judge. If the widow's persistent appeals to the unrighteous judge finally pressed him to action, how much more should we expect our greater God, who is righteous and loves his children, to hear our prayers and answer? It is not saying that God is like an unrighteous judge.

In verse one Luke gives us two reasons Jesus taught this parable to the disciples. First, "that they ought always pray." God never tires of hearing our prayers. Secondly, we should not "lose heart". The words *lose heart* mean to grow weary, which could happen if God doesn't answer our prayers right away. So, what God is saying is, even when we don't get an immediate response, we should not give up because God never tires of hearing our prayers.

Talk about It

▶ What does Jesus want his disciples to learn from this parable? *(He wants them to know they should always pray and never give up or grow weary of praying.)*

▶ Should we compare God to the unrighteous judge in the parable? *(We need to be careful not to say God is like an unrighteous judge. Remember the lesser and greater. If the lesser—the unrighteous judge, will listen to the woman's plea, how much more will the greater—God, hear our plea.)*

▶ What does God think about us asking him for the same things over and over again? Does he ever get tired of us asking? *(God never tires of hearing our prayers. Whenever we ask God to help us we trusting that he is all-powerful. That brings glory to God. Even though God does not always give us what we ask for, it brings him great joy for us to depend on him.)*

Pray about It

Pray that God gives you faith to persist in your prayers, trusting that he hears them and will answer.

Going Deeper

One day, all our prayers for healing will be answered. In that day, when Jesus returns, God will heal every sickness. On that day, all our prayers for relief against sin will be satisfied, and sin will finally and forever be destroyed. When Jesus, the Son of Man, returns, he will put an end to all sickness, pain, suffering, injustice and sin, and death. God hears our prayers and we can have confidence that he will act, but that may not come in our timing.

Ultimately, God will faithfully answer all our prayers. Though we suffer in our time here on earth, there will be no suffering in heaven. In the meantime, God uses it for our good, to strengthen our faith. So we must persevere in prayer. The sad ending to this parable is Jesus's question—when he comes again, will he find faith on the earth—or will he find that people have lost hope?

In this present age, our suffering can feel endless. But it is only temporary. Once we experience our ultimate healing in heaven, we will realize just how brief our earthly lives really were. For though we suffer occasionally here on earth, we will live eternally (forever) in the absence of pain, sin and sorrow.

Day Five

Listen Up

Read Matthew 6:7–13:

> *"And when you pray, do not heap up empty phrases as the Gentiles do, for they think that they will be heard for their many words. Do not be like them, for your Father knows what you need before you ask him. Pray then like this: 'Our Father in heaven, hallowed be your name. Your kingdom come, your will be done, on earth as it is in heaven. Give us this day our daily bread, and forgive us our debts, as we also have forgiven our debtors. And lead us not into temptation, but deliver us from evil.'"*

Think about It

We are ending this week the same place we began, by looking at the Lord's Prayer. This version of the prayer, given to us by Matthew, is part of a larger second teaching on prayer Jesus gave to his disciples. Jesus often repeated what he taught. He was a good teacher and knew that hearing things over again would help the disciples to learn.

When we compare the Lord's Prayer in Matthew with that of Luke, we notice several differences. The Lord's Prayer here in Matthew is longer. Instead of praying, "Father, hallowed be thy name," Jesus added the words "our" and "in heaven." How wonderful to be able to call God our Father. Matthew recorded the additional line, "Your will be done, on earth as it is in heaven" when praying for the kingdom to come. To close the prayer, Jesus added," but deliver us from evil."

The most encouraging part of all, doesn't come from these additions; it comes from the added instruction, "your Father knows what you need before you ask him." What an amazing truth. Jesus taught that we do not need to babble endless phrases and repeat our prayers countless times. We simply need to ask our Father, for he knows what we need, even before we speak it out in prayer.

In C.S. Lewis's book the Magician's Nephew, Polly and Digory are hungry and wonder why Aslan (he represents God) isn't giving them something to eat. Their horse Fledge suggests they ask. Polly questions, "wouldn't he know without being asked?" Fledge replies, "I've no doubt he would but I've a sort of idea he likes to be asked." Think about it. We ask God because we know he is all-powerful and that brings him glory. Always remember God is our Father, who loves to give good gifts to his children (Matthew 7:11).

We learned from our parables this week that God is glad to hear our prayers and provide for what we need. He is our Father in heaven, eager to listen to the prayers of his children. Best of all, God knows what we need, even before we ask.

Talk about It

▶ What are three prayers you can pray? *(Parents, you can teach your children to write down their requests on index cards or in a prayer journal so that they can remember what to pray each day. When God answers one of their prayers, they can write how God answered their prayer on the back of the card or in their prayer journal. Over time, reviewing these answered prayers helps build our faith for the new challenges that come our way.)*

▶ Have your upper elementary age children compare the two versions of the Lord's Prayer from Luke 11:2–5 and Matthew 6:9–13. Name the differences you can see. *(Parents, you can skip this exercise with younger children. We just covered the differences in the lesson above, but this exercise will help your children learn that they can compare two passages of Scripture and provide the needed repetition to help them to learn. While they may remember one of the above outlined differences, they probably would not remember them all unless they compare the passages. Also, there are a few wording differences that are not mentioned above. See if you can help them discover what they are.)*

▶ What is so encouraging about seeing the word *our* before the word *Father* in the prayer Jesus gave for us to pray? *(When Jesus adds the word* our *in the prayer, he is letting us know that God is not just his Father, God is our Father too. Think of it this way. Who would you feel more comfortable asking for money, your own father, or a stranger? Of course, you would have way more confidence your own father would provide what you need. In the same way, we should pray with confidence because our God is our Father.)*

▶ How can God possibly know what we need before we ask? *(God knows all things. That's hard for us to grasp, but that's part of what makes God, God. Look up the following verses to see how the Bible describes God's omniscience: Psalm 139:4, Psalm 147:4–5, Hebrews 4:13, 1 John 3:20.)*

Pray about It

Thank God for being our Father and loving us as his children. Praise God that he knows what we need before we ask.

Going Deeper

Did you ever wish there were more examples of prayer in the Bible? What most people don't realize is that many of the Psalms are prayers put to music. Consider the opening verses of Psalm 25:

> "To you, O Lord, I lift up my soul. O my God, in you I trust; let me not be put to shame; let not my enemies exult over me. Indeed, none who wait for you shall be put to shame; they shall be ashamed who are wantonly treacherous. Make me to know your ways, O Lord; teach me your paths. Lead me in your truth and teach me, for you are the God of my salvation; for you I wait all the day long" (Psalm 25:1–5).

In addition to praying through the Lord's Prayer, we can also pray through the Psalms. Praying through Psalm 25 might go something like this: "God, today I place my trust in you. Even though I am going through difficulties and some are against me, I know you can put my enemies to shame. While I wait for your deliverance help me to know your ways and how I should relate to those who are against me. While I wait for you to answer my prayer, teach me your ways and help me to live in a way that pleases and honors you."

Look up the following Old Testament passages to learn more about prayer:

- ▶ Hannah's Prayer (1 Samuel 1)
- ▶ Daniel's Confession (Daniel 9:1–19)
- ▶ Habakkuk's Song of Praise (Habakkuk 3)
- ▶ Jehoshaphat's Plea (2 Chronicles 20:5–12)

Week 8

Where Do You Store Your Treasure?

Let's Look at the Week. . .

While some people think money is a private matter and don't like hearing about it in church, Jesus talked a lot about money. Several of his parables address the topic. It is said that there are about 500 verses in the Bible about prayer, but nearly 2000 verses about money and the sins related to abusing money, like greed and covetousness.

Money itself is not evil. Jesus used money to buy food and pay taxes. Money is not the problem; the love of money is. You won't find money on any sin list in the Bible, but you will find the love of money listed as a sin in several places. The most familiar are found in Paul's first letter to Timothy. Paul writes, "For the love of money is a root of all kinds of evils. It is through this craving that some have wandered away from the faith and pierced themselves with many pangs" (1 Timothy 6:10).

This week we will spend our time discussing the Parable of the Rich Fool and the surrounding verses and answer the question, "Where is the best place for me to store up treasure, in heaven or on earth?"

Get Ready

The action word of the week is give.

We use the word *give* when passing something to someone. For instance, when your brother asks you to hand him a napkin at dinner, you *give* him a napkin. If you are sick with a cold, your mom might say, "Don't kiss your little sister, you might *give* her your cold." So you can *give* people good things and bad.

The kind of giving we are studying this week is the gift kind of giving. When we share a gift with someone, we offer it for free. We don't make the person pay for the gift. We carry out this same concept of giving when we help the poor, share our belongings and time with others, and offer our money and resources to God.

This week we will learn that God is the most generous giver of all so we can trust him to give us what we need, and follow his example in sharing what we have with others.

Which Jar Do You Want?

(The goal of this activity is to help your children recognize where they put their treasure.)

Supplies:

- Three clear pint size jars
- Thirty, one dollar bills
- Three sticky notes (Place a cross on one, a simple drawing of a house on the second, and a simple drawing of a car on the third.)

Before you gather your children for this object lesson, loosely crumple up the dollar bills and place them in one of the jars. The goal is to try and make the jar look full of money. Place the jars in a row and then call your children to view them.

Once your children arrive ask them a simple question: "If you could have one of these three jars, which one would you choose?" Now your children will of course pick the jar with the money. After they point to that jar ask them, "Why did you choose the jar with the money?" (They will likely tell you because money has value.)

Then empty the jar with the money and place a sticky note on each of the three jars. Explain to the children the cross represents God and his church, the house represents a big house, and the car, a fast car.

Tell them Jesus taught a proverb about how we spend our money. He said, "where your treasure is, there will your heart be also" (Luke 12:34). The proverb tells us that we are going to love the things we invest in. Then put all the money into the jar marked "house." Ask your children, "If you put all your money into buying a house, what do you think you are going to love?" (They should say the house.) Do the same for the car.

Finally take the money back out and say, "But what happens if you don't get such a big house (place eight of the dollars into the house)? What if you get a regular, ordinary car (place five more of the dollars into the car jar)? If you give the rest to the church, serving God, and helping others (place the rest of the money in the jar with the cross), what are you going to love the most?" (Your children should answer the church or God.) Then you can explain that God knows we need to use our money for a home and for transportation and other things like food and clothes, but God also knows that when we are rich toward him, using our money to bless the church and others, our love for both will flourish. This week we are going to study the topic of money and the best place to store our treasure.

Day One

Listen Up

Read Luke 12:13–15:

> *Someone in the crowd said to him, "Teacher, tell my brother to divide the inheritance with me." But he said to him, "Man, who made me a judge or arbitrator over you?" And he said to them, "Take care, and be on your guard against all covetousness, for one's life does not consist in the abundance of his possessions."*

Think about It

Kids appeal to their parents to settle arguments all the time. Have you ever had a disagreement with your brother or sister and called to your parent, "Tell Bobbie to give me back the ball. I had it first!" Sound familiar? One day, while Jesus was teaching the crowd, a man called out to Jesus and asked him to act as a judge between him and his brother in a similar way. It appears from his complaint that his father died, and now he was in an argument with his older brother over his inheritance. An inheritance is the money and possessions that are passed onto the children when their father dies. Inheritance could be a property like a house, or it could be a sum of money. It was common in Israel for the older brother to get a larger share of the inheritance than his younger brother. The man bringing the complaint is likely the unhappy younger brother who is asking Jesus to tell his older brother to split the money equally, so they both get an equal share. He doesn't like getting less.

One thing we see is that the younger brother is more interested in money than grieving over the loss of his father. Also, it seems clear that he did not come to hear Jesus teach, like the rest of the crowd. He interrupted Jesus's teaching and demanded that Jesus tell his brother to give him an equal share. Jesus refused to take up the man's case but did address the topic of greed and the dangers of covetousness—that is, wanting something that belongs to someone else.

Did you ever want something that didn't belong to you? Like when your friend had a birthday party and received the exact toy you had wanted? As soon as you saw it, you knew that your parents could never afford to buy you such a gift. How did you feel when you then realized you would never get something like that? Did you ever get angry over not having something?

Coveting seems OK—wanting what you don't have doesn't seem as bad as stealing or murder for instance. But we need to remember that loving the things of the world fills the same space in our heart that we are supposed to fill with a love for God. You can see, when we love and desire the things of the world instead of God or more than God, this is sinful. Coveting is a sin we all struggle with, but that doesn't make it OK. A godly desire for something draws us close to God—to ask him for what we need. The sinful desire of coveting makes us angry with God and others when we don't get what we want.

Talk about It

▶ What is coveting? *(Coveting is the desire for something that does not belong to you. If your shoes wear out, it is natural to want a new pair. But if you experience anger toward someone else who is wearing new shoes, and wish you could have their shoes, you are experiencing covetousness. While a godly desire for something draws us close to God—to ask him for what we need, the sinful desire of coveting produces anger toward God and others because we don't have what we want. Covetousness steals our joy.)*

▶ How can you tell the difference between a godly desire and coveting? *(It is OK to want something. We want to have food when we get hungry for instance. We want a new pair of shoes when our old ones wear out. But when we want something so much that it steals our joy or makes us ungrateful or angry, we have probably fallen into the sin of coveting.)*

▶ Can you think of something you coveted—something that you wanted that did not belong to you? *(Parents, take this opportunity to share something you have coveted. Coveting is a very common sin—a sin we often commit every day. Television commercials entice us to want things that we do not need or can't afford to buy. We can also covet things that our family, friends, and neighbors have.)*

Pray about It

Ask God for help in confessing the sin of coveting and strength to love him more than anything else in the world.

Going Deeper

There is nothing sinful about needing an item you don't have, like when you are baking a cake and you run out of eggs. In that moment your desire for eggs hits the roof, as you scour the fridge for a hidden egg that of course you know is not there. There is nothing sinful about admiring an item, like a beautiful painting. Still you must be aware that the sin of coveting loves to hitch a ride upon our desires. A good indicator of covetousness is when the desire steals your joy. If not owning something makes you angry or robs you of peace, you have likely fallen into covetousness. (The sin Jesus mentions in our Bible passage, coveting, is a strong desire for something you don't have but want. Coveting can tempt a person to steal what doesn't belong to them or to say bad things about the person who has what they don't have.

In the case of our Bible story, the younger brother wanted an equal share of his father's money and got angry when his older brother got a larger portion. The younger brother coveted an equal share. While Jesus didn't give the man what he wanted, his teaching to, "be on your guard against covetousness," was exactly what the angry man needed to hear.

The sin of coveting is the great equalizer—everybody falls into this sin. Not everyone has committed adultery, not everyone has stolen, but everyone covets. Coveting is what got Eve in trouble as she looked at the forbidden fruit and desired it, then disobeyed. The Apostle Paul described the sin of coveting as such a common part of life that had the Law not said, do not covet (Romans 7:7), he wouldn't have known it was a sin. Our children are taught and enticed to covet nearly every day. If you help them to understand coveting as a sin, you will help them see their need for a Savior over the things of the world.

Day Two

Listen Up

Read Luke 12:16–21:

> *And he told them a parable, saying, "The land of a rich man produced plentifully, and he thought to himself, 'What shall I do, for I have nowhere to store my crops?' And he said, 'I will do this: I will tear down my barns and build larger ones, and there I will store all my grain and my goods. And I will say to my soul, "Soul, you have ample goods laid up for many years; relax, eat, drink, be merry."' But God said to him, 'Fool! This night your soul is required of you, and the things you have prepared, whose will they be?' So is the one who lays up treasure for himself and is not rich toward God."*

Think about It

The rich man in our story was greedy; he wanted all the crops for himself. He didn't bless his laborers with a bonus. There is no record of him giving a tenth (a tithe) back to God. There is no mention of any concern for the poor or even sharing it with family and friends. He wanted to sit back, relax and party and keep it all for himself.

The man was not grateful for all that God had given him. When God provides abundantly (gives us a lot) our hearts should fill up with thankfulness. We use the word *gratitude* to describe that feeling of thankfulness. Gratitude (thankfulness for all God gave us) leads to generosity (abundant giving to others). You see, when God gives us much, we should share it with others who are in need. But if we lack gratitude, we never feel as though we have enough and then we become stingy, keeping all that we have for ourselves.

Finally, the man thought he was in control of his life; his future was all planned. He would tear down his existing barns—note that he has more than one. Then build new, larger barns. The whole process could take months. Once complete, the man reasoned, he would have everything he needed for many years. But God interrupted the man's plans and brought his life to an abrupt end. The man thought he was in control, but the story shows us that he didn't have any control. It is God who controls all things.

Jesus ended the parable with a warning, that if we are greedy, like the man in the parable and are not rich toward God, we will suffer his same fate. Perhaps the young man who demanded Jesus act upon his older brother was still there to hear Jesus share this parable. If so, was he wise enough to listen up, and give up his fight to get what did not belong to him? Unfortunately, Jesus didn't give us the rest of his story.

Talk about It

▶ What mistake did the rich fool make? *(The rich fool was greedy. Instead of returning some of his harvest to God or blessing God's people, he wanted to keep it all for himself. He was not grateful or thankful for what God gave him. As a result, he became stingy instead of generous.)*

▶ Have you ever struggled with the sin of greed—wanting to keep things all for yourself? *(Parents, share a time when you experienced greed. Perhaps you didn't want to share or lend something to another person in need.)*

▶ What are some ways we can be rich toward God? *(We can share our things with God's people or give a tenth (tithe) of our income to the church. We can bless our neighbors or give to the poor. All these demonstrate a love for God or the people he created.)*

Pray about It

Ask God to reveal any greed in your own heart and for strength to be generous with your harvest.

Going Deeper

After refusing to act on the man's complaint against his brother, Jesus turned to the crowd and shared the Parable of the Rich Fool. He wanted to be sure they understood how greed affects the way we live. Greed is a selfish desire to keep or have something for yourself and not share it with others. Think of the little boy whose mom gave him a brand new pack of gum. When his sister asked for a piece, he refused because he wanted to keep it all for himself. The boy's desire to keep it all for himself demonstrates that the sin of greed is at work in his heart.

There are several interesting details to the rich man described in the parable. First, the man is not a farmer. Jesus didn't say, "the land of a farmer produced a bountiful harvest." A farmer works his land while the landowner pays others to do the labor. In this parable, it appears we have a rich landowner who sat back while his workers took care of everything. Also, it is interesting to notice that Jesus says the land produced the crop, not the rich man. The Bible teaches that a man can plant and cultivate, but only God can make something grow (1 Corinthians 3:7).

Day Three

Listen Up

Read Luke 12:22–26:

> *And he said to his disciples, "Therefore I tell you, do not be anxious about your life, what you will eat, nor about your body, what you will put on. For life is more than food, and the body more than clothing. Consider the ravens: they neither sow nor reap, they have neither storehouse nor barn, and yet God feeds them. Of how much more value are you than the birds! And which of you by being anxious can add a single hour to his span of life? If then you are not able to do as small a thing as that, why are you anxious about the rest?*

Think about It

After sharing the Parable of the Rich Fool, Jesus turned to his disciples to encourage them. Jesus wanted the disciples, who had given everything up to follow him, to know that they could trust God to provide for their needs. The disciples did not have to worry or be anxious about food or clothing or any other basic requirement. God would take care of those things.

Think of the man in the last parable. Jesus described him as a rich man. But notice what the man said to himself after the enormous harvest came in—"Soul, you have ample goods laid up for many years; relax." Why did he need to "relax?" Perhaps it was because his riches could not satisfy him. His money could not keep him from worrying about his future. Even though he was rich, he felt like he needed more. If you do not trust God to provide what you need, you will always be afraid of running out or not having enough.

Jesus presented two word pictures to help the disciples trust God for their needs. The first is God providing food for the ravens. Although ravens love juniper berries, you never see them planting rows of juniper trees in a field. They also don't store extra juniper berries up for the future. Ravens don't worry about where their next meal will come from—God provides it. If God provides for the birds, how much more will he provide for us, his children.

We live abundant lives. Our grocery store shelves are packed with food. We can usually buy what we like, and we have refrigerators to keep our food from spoiling. But it is not like that everywhere around the world. Those living in harsh climates rely on farming. They don't have refrigerators. The store shelves are stocked with only the basics, and even those are quite expensive. When you live in a place where you depend on crops and climates, the word picture of the ravens is all the more applicable, and it encourages us to trust God for our physical needs.

When Jesus taught this parable to the disciples, they didn't know he was going to die on the cross for their sins. That hadn't happened yet. But when we read this parable we know God gave us the greatest gift of all when he sent his Son Jesus to die for our sins (John 3:16). If God would give up his only Son for us, to die on the cross, then surely he will provide for our daily needs.

Talk about It

▶ What is the greatest gift God has given us? *(God gave us his only Son to die in our place so that we could be forgiven.)*

▶ How can remembering that God sent his only Son, help us to trust him for smaller things like food and clothing? *(If God was willing to give us his only Son, he must be willing to give us the smaller things we need.)*

▶ Why are ravens a good example of how the Lord provides? *(The ravens don't think about what they are going to eat tomorrow. Yet each day God provides for them. We should be like the ravens and trust God or our daily needs.)*

▶ Can you think of a time when you worried about not having enough food or clothes to wear? *(Parents, your children may not be able to think of a time when they worried about these things in particular. Remind them of how wonderfully God has provided for their needs. If they do have a story, allow them to share, or you can remember one from your life. Take time to share and talk about it.)*

Pray about It

Thank God for providing the clothing, food, and shelter that we need.

Going Deeper

When God blesses us with abundance, it is easy to think we received our prosperity because we worked for it and forget that it is God who provided for us. Prior to the Israelites entering the Promised Land, God gave them a warning that also applies to our hearts today. He warned against the effects of covetousness. Consider these words:

> "Take care lest you forget the LORD your God by not keeping his commandments and his rules and his statutes, which I command you today, lest, when you have eaten and are full and have built good houses and live in them, and when your herds and flocks multiply and your silver and gold is multiplied and all that you have is multiplied, then your heart be lifted up, and you forget the LORD your God, who brought you out of the land of Egypt, out of the house of slavery, who led you through the great and terrifying wilderness, with its fiery serpents and scorpions and thirsty ground where there was no water, who brought you water out of the flinty rock, who fed you in the wilderness with manna that your fathers did not know, that he might humble you and test you, to do you good in the end. Beware lest you say in your heart, 'My power and the might of my hand have gotten me this wealth.' You shall remember the LORD your God, for it is he who gives you power to get wealth, that he may confirm his covenant that he swore to your fathers, as it is this day" (Deuteronomy 8:11–18).

Day Four

Listen Up

Read Luke 12:27–31:

> *Consider the lilies, how they grow: they neither toil nor spin, yet I tell you, even Solomon in all his glory was not arrayed like one of these. But if God so clothes the grass, which is alive in the field today, and tomorrow is thrown into the oven, how much more will he clothe you, O you of little faith! And do not seek what you are to eat and what you are to drink, nor be worried. For all the nations of the world seek after these things, and your Father knows that you need them. Instead, seek his kingdom, and these things will be added to you.*

The lilies referred to by Jesus are not the same flower we call lilies in the west. The flower Jesus was speaking of is a type of red poppy native to Palestine that sprouts after the spring rains in Israel. Its Latin name is Anemone Coronaria. The poppy flowers bloom by the millions, covering the fields with a breathtaking sea of scarlet. They grow wild and spread naturally without the help of a gardener. The disciples would have been very familiar with these flowers. To become more familiar yourself, search the Internet for "photos of Anemoney Coronaria blooming in Palestine."

Think about It

Jesus used the image of flowers blooming to help the disciples trust God for their physical needs. If God provides such a beautiful covering for grass, how much more will he provide for his children. God's people are worth more than grass to him.

Word pictures help us remember what Jesus taught. From that day forward, every spring when the disciples saw the fields of poppies bloom, they remembered that there was no need to worry. The same can be true for us. Whenever we see beautiful blooming flowers in a field, we can remember that God cares for us and will provide for our needs.

Jesus ends this word picture with a charge, "seek his kingdom, and these things will be added to you" (Luke 12:31). The disciples had given up everything to follow Jesus, and he wanted them to know that his Father was aware of their needs and would provide for them. But he added one condition, that the disciples must first seek the kingdom. Seeking the kingdom meant seeking to expand God's rule over the earth—and it naturally resulted in the expansion of the kingdom of God in their own lives. Jesus challenged them to hold nothing back, but rather to love and follow him with every part of their being. He also called the disciples to tell others about him, which led to the expansion of God's kingdom in the lives of others. Everything that Jesus taught them, also applies to us (Matthew 28:20).

Jesus's charge is familiar to David's in Psalm 34: "Oh, taste and see that the LORD is good! Blessed is the man who takes refuge in him! Oh, fear the LORD, you his saints, for those who fear him have no lack! The young lions suffer want and hunger; but those who seek the LORD lack no good thing" (Psalms 34:8–10).

Talk about It

▶ How could a field full of flowers encourage the disciples not to worry about the things they needed? *(If God clothes the grass so beautifully—and it is only grass, how much more will he provide clothing for his children.)*

▶ Jesus said not to worry about our needs because the Father knows them all. Do you remember a verse from last week that teaches something similar? *(In last week's lesson on prayer we learned that "your Father knows what you need before you ask him" [Matthew 6:8].)*

▶ What does it mean to seek God's kingdom? *(God's kingdom is his rule and reign over the earth. Each time we read God's Word to learn more about him, we are seeking the kingdom. Each time we follow the Bible's teaching, we are seeking God's kingdom. So, by going through this study to learn, you are seeking God's kingdom.)*

Pray about It

Ask God to help you seek his kingdom and help you grow in your desire to obey and follow him.

Going Deeper

A great illustration of God's ability to provide is Jesus's miraculous multiplication of fish and bread to feed the crowds that followed him. Jesus fed the multitudes twice. We read the first account in Mark 6 where Jesus fed five thousand. He took five loaves and two fish and ended up with twelve baskets of leftovers. Then later in Mark 8, Jesus multiplies seven loaves to feed four thousand people, with seven baskets full of leftovers.

We can read these stories and say to ourselves, "Yes Jesus multiplied the fish miraculously, but that was then. Jesus isn't around anymore to provide for my needs." It is true that Jesus is not here to multiply fish and loaves to meet our needs, but we should also not too quickly dismiss God's ability or desire to provide in miraculous ways. There are countless stories of God providing what people needed—at just the right time.

When we read stories like the miraculous multiplication of fishes and loaves, we are not supposed to try and recreate the miracle. But we're also not supposed to relegate the entire story to history. We need to remember that the same God who multiplied the fishes and loaves, lives within us and is able to provide for us in ways we could never think or imagine.

Day Five

Listen Up

Read Luke 12:32–34:

> *"Fear not, little flock, for it is your Father's good pleasure to give you the kingdom. Sell your possessions, and give to the needy. Provide yourselves with moneybags that do not grow old, with a treasure in the heavens that does not fail, where no thief approaches and no moth destroys. For where your treasure is, there will your heart be also."*

Think about It

Jesus's encouragement in our passage today is similar to that in his Sermon on the Mount. While teaching on the mountain Jesus said, "Do not lay up for yourselves treasures on earth, where moth and rust destroy and where thieves break in and steal, but lay up for yourselves treasures in heaven, where neither moth nor rust destroys and where thieves do not break in and steal" (Matthew 6:19–20).

"You can't take it with you" is a popular phrase about money and possessions. It is meant to encourage a person to spend their money now and enjoy life because we can't take our money with us after we die. The rich fool had a similar philosophy. He wanted to store up treasure for himself on earth so that he could, "eat, drink, and be merry" (Luke 12:19). In other words, he wanted to live his life working to earn money to party. Parties are fun, but we're not supposed to spend all our money on ourselves. God gives us money so that out of thanks for him we will share our abundance with others. You see, when you realize that our real party will be in heaven with Jesus, it is much easier to give away what you have with others in need.

Jesus presented this idea to the man. He said that when we give our money or possessions to help the needy, we are storing up treasure in heaven. Jesus called it a moneybag that would not grow old" (Luke 12:33). But what if you give your money away to the poor and then run into trouble yourself? Well, once you understand that God provides everything you need (like the ravens and the lilies of the field) then it is easier to give your money away to the poor. If you are worried and are not sure you will have enough money for tomorrow (like the rich fool), you are more likely to keep what you have and still want more.

What about you? Do you have an abundance of possessions? How many shirts do you have? How many toys, games, bikes, scooters and sports items do you have? There are a lot of kids in the world who only have one or two shirts, one toy if they are fortunate. Have you ever considered giving something you own to someone in need? If so, you too can store up treasures in heaven.

Talk about It

▶ How can you get treasure in heaven? *(We can't take our money with us, but we can send it ahead as treasure by using our money to help the needy and giving it away to the poor.)*

▶ How are our heart and money related? *(Where we spend our money reveals what we love in our heart and can cause our love for something to grow. If we invest in the mission of the church, we will grow to love the mission of the church.)*

▶ Can you think of a way that you could store up treasure in heaven? *(Parents, help your children answer this question. Do they have a job where they earn money and tithe or give to missions? Do they have an abundance of things they could use to bless others in need? Also, take time to review your own life. Are you giving to the poor and the mission of the church?)*

Pray about It

Ask God to help you grow in the grace of giving, and trust him to provide all that you need to be a blessing to others.

Going Deeper

Jesus ended his teaching by reminding the disciples that where your treasure is there will your heart be also. In other words, our spending reveals what we love. If you invest all your money into horses, you show that you love horses, and if you spend all your money on a fancy car, then it is clear that you love your car the most. But it is also true that we can cultivate a love for something by investing in it. For example, if we give our money to the needy and see their faces light up with gratitude, our hearts will be moved. When we give our money to the church, and then see how the church helps others, our affection for the church will grow.

Pull out your checkbook register and do a survey by reviewing the pages and asking yourself, "What do I love?" If you had to gauge what you love by how you spend your money, what does your spending reveal? Now of course we really don't love the electric company or car repair shop—and they can take a ton of our cash. But, how much are you paying each month to credit card bills? Do we really need everything we think we need? How much are you giving to the church or missions? Be encouraged to love God and trust his provision for you. Is he prompting you to make any changes?

Week 9

You Are Invited to the Banquet

Let's Look at the Week. . .

This week we'll study the parables of Luke 14. Jesus told these parables on the Sabbath to a gathering of religious rulers. It was customary for the Jews in Jesus's day to eat a meal together after celebrating the Sabbath. Today, Christian families often enjoy a similar time of hospitality after church.

As our story opens, Jesus arrives at the house of the ruling Pharisee to share a meal on the Sabbath. But this is no friendly time of hospitality. The host of the banquet was planning to trap Jesus and has invited his Pharisee friends to join him. As part of their scheme, they welcomed in a sick man, suffering from dropsy (edema). What the man had was not contagious, so the Pharisees were not breaking any rules, yet the man's swollen limbs were obvious to all. They wanted to see if they could provoke Jesus to heal on the Sabbath and then accuse him of working on the day of rest.

Get Ready

The action word of the week is come.

The moment you receive an invitation in the mail you have a choice to make. The invitation is asking, "will you come?" You must decide if you will accept or decline. The Parable of the Banquet, which we will study later in the week, illustrates the invitation the Bible gives to us all. The Scriptures invite us to come to Jesus and believe in him. In John 7:37–38 we read, "On the last day of the feast, the great day, Jesus stood up and cried out, 'If anyone thirsts, let him come to me and drink. Whoever believes in me, as the Scripture has said, "Out of his heart will flow rivers of living water."'" Jesus also said:

> *"I am the bread of life; whoever comes to me shall not hunger, and whoever believes in me shall never thirst. But I said to you that you have seen me and yet do not believe. All that the Father gives me will come to me, and whoever comes to me I will never cast out. For I have come down from heaven, not to do my own will but the will of him*

who sent me. And this is the will of him who sent me, that I should lose nothing of all that he has given me, but raise it up on the last day. For this is the will of my Father, that everyone who looks on the Son and believes in him should have eternal life, and I will raise him up on the last day" (John 6:35–40).

So, we are all invited to come to Jesus and believe. Sadly, not everyone who is invited is willing to come.

Imagine You Are Ten Feet Tall

(The goal of this activity is to demonstrate pride.)

Supplies:

- A chair or ladder
- A flat sheet
- A large safety pin or binder clip

Explain that we use the word *pride* for a person who boasts about themselves, or for a person who thinks they are more important than others. An easy way to describe pride is the belief that you are superior to others.

To illustrate this, line everybody up from tallest to shortest to determine your order by height. Then set up the ladder and help the shortest person up the steps. (If you don't have a ladder, have them stand on the chair holding the chair back for stability.) Wrap the sheet around their shoulders like a cloak to hide the ladder and fasten it around their neck with the safety pin or clip.

Ask them how it feels to be taller than everyone else. Does it make them feel more powerful? Does it make them feel more important?

The sin of pride works like the ladder. Though we are short, it fools us into thinking we are taller, more powerful, or greater than others.

Provide each child with a chance to stand on the ladder act proud. They could make arrogant statements like, "Look at me! I'm the tallest person in the house. I am superior and tower over you."

Day One

Listen Up

Read Luke 14:1–6:

> *One Sabbath, when he went to dine at the house of a ruler of the Pharisees, they were watching him carefully. And behold, there was a man before him who had dropsy. And Jesus responded to the lawyers and Pharisees, saying, "Is it lawful to heal on the Sabbath, or not?" But they remained silent. Then he took him and healed him and sent him away. And he said to them, "Which of you, having a son or an ox that has fallen into a well on a Sabbath day, will not immediately pull him out?" And they could not reply to these things.*

Think about It

Following the service at the temple, the Pharisees invited Jesus to a meal to see if he would heal the sick man who they also welcomed in. If Jesus healed the man, they would accuse him of breaking the Law by working on the Sabbath. But Jesus wasn't fooled by the trap they set for him, for religious leaders had accused him of working on the Sabbath before. Earlier in his ministry, Jesus healed a woman on the Sabbath. Luke recorded the story: "the ruler of the synagogue, indignant because Jesus had healed on the Sabbath, said to the people, "There are six days in which work ought to be done. Come on those days and be healed, and not on the Sabbath day" (Luke 13:14).

So in this case, Jesus decided to confront the issue head on and ask, "Is it lawful to heal on the Sabbath?" The Pharisees didn't expect the question and were afraid to answer.

Jesus then challenged the Pharisees by giving them an illustration of an ox falling in a ditch. Jesus knew the Pharisees saw saving an animal as an exception to the no work on the Sabbath rule. If the Pharisees agreed that it was lawful to rescue an ox on the Sabbath, why would it be any different to heal (rescue) the man from his sickness? But the Pharisees again were silent. Their double standard was exposed—it was OK for them to rescue an ox, but not OK for Jesus to heal.

Remember our warm-up from this week? The rules the Pharisees made and followed religiously, served as their ladder. They looked down upon others who could not keep their added rules, though inside they were sinners like the rest. The Pharisees also looked down on Jesus, thinking they were greater when in fact Jesus was the sinless Son of God. They didn't think they needed to come to Jesus, so they trusted in their ability to keep the Law.

Talk about It

▶ Why did the Pharisees invite the man with dropsy to come to the meal? *(They wanted to trap Jesus to see if he would heal the man.)*

▶ Do you think the Pharisees believed Jesus could heal? If so, why didn't they follow him? *(Yes, the Pharisees knew Jesus healed people, that's why they invited the man with dropsy. They didn't follow Jesus because they thought they were greater than him. They wanted to be in charge and wanted the people to follow them, not Jesus.)*

▶ Can you think of a time in your life when you thought you were greater or better than someone else? *(Parents, help your children by sharing a time in your life when you thought you were better than someone else. Then help your children think of a time when they demonstrated pride.)*

Pray about It

Ask God to help you battle against pride so that you will not look down on others, but rather treat them with love.

Going Deeper

The Pharisees were proud men. They made up a ton of rules about what the Jews could and could not do on the Sabbath. The Pharisees kept these man-made rules religiously and criticized anyone who did not follow them. God's Law did say that his people should rest on the seventh day, but it did not forbid healing on the Sabbath—that rule was one the Pharisees added.

In addition to the Ten Commandments, there are over 600 additional commandments in the Old Testament Law. These commandments governed everything from what you could eat to how to treat diseases. But the Pharisees added many more commandments to the Law in a book called the Midrash. The Midrash contained hundreds of commands to ensure you never broke one of God's commands. The Pharisees wanted to be able to know that they did not break the Law. God's command to keep the Sabbath holy by resting and not working was not clear enough for the Pharisees. They added 39 categories of work to make sure a person kept the command. They didn't deal with the heart, but they instead focused on externals.

Some of the categories of prohibited work are obvious, like plowing a field or harvesting a crop. But they took these to extremes and criticized Jesus and the disciples for gleaning grain to eat (Matthew 12:1–2). Other laws in the Midrash seemed ridiculous. For instance, you were permitted to write or erase one letter but not two. You could move an object from inside your house to outside, but not more than four cubits (six feet). So you could throw a bone to your dog, but you better be careful that it not roll seven feet or you would be guilty of doing work on the Sabbath.

Day Two

Listen Up

Read Luke 14:7–11:

> *Now he told a parable to those who were invited, when he noticed how they chose the places of honor, saying to them, "When you are invited by someone to a wedding feast, do not sit down in a place of honor, lest someone*

more distinguished than you be invited by him, and he who invited you both will come and say to you, 'Give your place to this person,' and then you will begin with shame to take the lowest place. But when you are invited, go and sit in the lowest place, so that when your host comes he may say to you, 'Friend, move up higher.' Then you will be honored in the presence of all who sit at table with you. For everyone who exalts himself will be humbled, and he who humbles himself will be exalted."

Think about It

It is a tradition at weddings to seat the bride and groom and their wedding party at a head table in the center of the wedding feast. The closer your table is to the head table, the more important you are. So the table reserved for the parents of the bride and groom is usually very close to the head table. Back in Jesus's day a similar tradition applied to any meal where you invited guests to your home. Three tables were set up in a U shape. The host and his most honored guest sat at the head table, the more important guests sat closer to the host. At this banquet, Jesus watched the religious rulers rush to grab the seats closest to the host. They wanted the seats of honor.

Jesus used the Parable of the Places of Honor to chide the Pharisees. As Jesus told the parable, you can imagine the men rethinking their choices of seats for they had only considered themselves. Still, none of them apologized or gave up their seats in response to Jesus's teaching.

Jesus ended the parable by sharing a truth found in Proverbs 29:23 which says, "One's pride will bring him low, but he who is lowly in spirit will obtain honor." Jesus explained that God is behind this principle. If you humble yourself before the Lord, he will exalt you. But if you exalt yourself, you will be brought low.

Imagine what it was like when the first of the invited guests arrived a bit early to see open seats at the head table. "Look at this, I am the first to arrive and have my choice of seats. I could take a seat at a side table, but then again, I think I deserve a seat at the head table. After all, I got here first. And who knows, I doubt there are any more important men to come. And even so, there are at least six seats at the table of honor. I will only take one of them."

Then the other religious rulers fought for positions of honor around the table as they rushed in to grab the best seats for themselves. But in thinking of themselves, they all missed the opportunity to give the place of honor to Jesus. Pride keeps our eyes focused on ourselves instead of upon God. Jesus was clear—"everyone who exalts himself will be humbled." God usually humbles us through failures and trial. So, why take the chance, knowing pride will eventually catch up with all of us? Take the humble seat and consider others more important than yourself.

Talk about It

▶ Can you think of ways we struggle with pride today—thinking we are better than others? *(Parents, you know your children, help them to see how they like to take the best seats in front of the TV or in the car. Most kids like sitting by the door in a car and not having to be in the middle, or climb into the back seat. Help your children see how this parable relates to them.)*

▶ What are some ways you can show humility toward others? When you think humility, think serving others and taking the lowest place. *(See if you can make a list of at least ten things your children can do to show humility toward others.)*

▶ How can we show humility toward God? *(Parents, you can explain to your children that humility is making yourself lower before someone who is greater. We show humility toward God by believing that he rules over us and by submitting to and obeying his Word. We demonstrate pride when we refuse to follow God's Word and do what we want instead.)*

Pray about It

Ask God to help you live a humble life before God and others.

Going Deeper

The disciples learned principles of humility from Jesus. After Jesus had ascended to heaven, they passed what they learned to us through their Epistles. Humility became a key teaching point for the disciples. James wrote, "Humble yourselves before the Lord, and he will exalt you" (James 4:10). Peter wrote, "Humble yourselves, therefore, under the mighty hand of God so that at the proper time he may exalt you" (1 Peter 5:6).

Both Peter and James learned the hard way. James, a brother of Jesus, didn't initially believe that Jesus was the Messiah (John 7:5); he thought Jesus was out of his mind (Mark 3:21). Peter boasted that he would never desert Jesus and soon after, denied three times he even knew the Lord. Prior to Jesus's death on the cross, all the disciples argued who among them was the greatest (Luke 9:46; 22:24). But after Jesus's death, the disciples were humbled for deserting Jesus, the one who went to the cross to pay for their sin.

Day Three

Listen Up

Read Luke 14:12–14:

> *He said also to the man who had invited him, "When you give a dinner or a banquet, do not invite your friends or your brothers or your relatives or rich neighbors, lest they also invite you in return and you be repaid. But when you give a feast, invite the poor, the crippled, the lame, the blind, and you will be blessed, because they cannot repay you. For you will be repaid at the resurrection of the just."*

Think about It

Jesus challenged the selfishness and pride of the guests for taking the best seats. All along, the ruler of the Pharisees, the host of the banquet, watched without objection. He knew Jesus was right. His friends did grab the best seats for themselves whenever they came to his gatherings. But Jesus wasn't finished. He had a parable for the host as well. You see, the host only invited the kind of people who made him look important or who would return the favor and invite him to one of their banquets. Rather than invite friends or the rich to a banquet, Jesus taught we should invite the poor and the lame—the ones who cannot pay us back or return the invitation.

Jesus knew that the ruler of the Pharisees didn't invite his guests for dinner to bless them, he invited people who he knew could return the favor. In other words, *I invite you to my party so that you will invite me to yours.* The only man he invited that could not return the blessing was the sick man, afflicted with dropsy. But we know that the only reason they invited him was to trap Jesus.

What about us? What is our motive for who we invite to our parties? Do we look to invite family and popular friends who will bring us gifts or in turn, invite us to their special events? Instead of judging the Pharisees too quickly, we should consider how often we are just like them. We are often tempted to avoid inviting the poor or unpopular people we know. So the challenge Jesus offered to the religious leaders is a good one for us to think about as well.

Talk about It

▶ Who did the Pharisees choose to invite to their dinners and parties? Who did they avoid inviting? *(The Pharisees invited the rich and the powerful—people who could return the blessing. They didn't invite the poor and needy.)*

▶ The ruler of the Pharisees did invite the man afflicted with dropsy. So why didn't Jesus compliment him for inviting the sick man? *(The ruler of the Pharisees didn't invite the man with dropsy to bless him, but rather to trap Jesus. After Jesus healed the sick man, the guests were only critical and did not celebrate his healing. Jesus knew the man was not welcome in that crowd, so he sent him away.)*

▶ Imagine you were hosting a party. Who are the friends you would want to invite and who are the people you might rather not invite? *(Parents, help your children think of people who represent the poor and lame in their lives. There may be a child with a learning disability or sickness that your child might rather not invite, or it could be someone who is not a part of the popular crowd.)*

The Pharisees were religious leaders in Jesus's day. They took pride in their ability to keep the law of Moses and set up even stricter laws than those given in the Bible. This way, they could prove that they never broke the Law. For example, in Deuteronomy 6:8 Moses says that the Law of God should be bound to your hand and placed as a frontlet between your eyes. This was a way of saying you should remember to keep the Law of God at all times.

But how do you ensure you are not breaking that law? The self-righteous Pharisees came up with an answer. They made small leather boxes called phylacteries and filled them with little scrolls of Scripture. They tied these boxes to their hands and foreheads and walked around proudly demonstrating their obedience to the Law. Jesus rebuked them for this outward behavior (Matthew 23:5). He said they looked good on the outside but inwardly were like tombs filled with dead men's bones because their hearts were far from God (Matthew 23:27).

Pray about It

Ask God to help you reach out to the less fortunate, not just those who can bless you in return. It is also important that we see ourselves as poor and needy before God. Pray that God pours out his grace on each person in your family so that each one will turn their heart toward him.

Going Deeper

Jesus was nothing like the Pharisees. When he multiplied the fishes and loaves, everyone was welcome to eat. Jesus reached out to the tax collectors and prostitutes and even ate in their homes. The following passage describes the criticism of the Pharisees:

> And as Jesus reclined at table in the house, behold, many tax collectors and sinners came and were reclining with Jesus and his disciples. And when the Pharisees saw this, they said to his disciples, "Why does your teacher eat with tax collectors and sinners?" But when he heard it, he said, "Those who are well have no need of a physician, but those who are sick. Go and learn what this means: 'I desire mercy, and not sacrifice.' For I came not to call the righteous, but sinners" (Matthew 9:10–13).

How different is Jesus's philosophy from that of the Pharisees? Jesus came to serve, not to be served. Jesus said, "the Son of Man came not to be served but to serve, and to give his life as a ransom for many" (Matthew 20:28).

Day Four

Listen Up

Read Luke 14:15–24:

> *When one of those who reclined at table with him heard these things, he said to him, "Blessed is everyone who will eat bread in the kingdom of God!" But he said to him, "A man once gave a great banquet and invited many. And at the time for the banquet he sent his servant to say to those who had been invited, 'Come, for everything is now ready.' But they all alike began to make excuses. The first said to him, 'I have bought a field, and I must go out and*

see it. Please have me excused.' And another said, 'I have bought five yoke of oxen, and I go to examine them. Please have me excused.' And another said, 'I have married a wife, and therefore I cannot come.' So the servant came and reported these things to his master. Then the master of the house became angry and said to his servant, 'Go out quickly to the streets and lanes of the city, and bring in the poor and crippled and blind and lame.' And the servant said, 'Sir, what you commanded has been done, and still there is room.' And the master said to the servant, 'Go out to the highways and hedges and compel people to come in, that my house may be filled. For I tell you, none of those men who were invited shall taste my banquet.'"

Think about It

One of the guests reclining at the table with Jesus spoke out. He connected Jesus's teaching to the great feast we will one day enjoy in heaven. The man shouted, "Blessed is everyone who will eat bread in the kingdom of God!" It is clear from his comment that he assumed he would go to heaven to enjoy the feast. But what he didn't realize is that he had already rejected the invitation. Like those who gave excuses in the parable, he missed his opportunity by rejecting Jesus and trying to trap him. Sin makes us all poor and needy before God, no matter how much we have or how well we think we have done.

The servant in the parable who announced the invitation to the banquet is a picture of Jesus. God the Father sent his Son into the world to die on the cross for our sin and to spread the good news that everyone who trusts in his work upon the cross will join in his heavenly banquet. So, if you reject Jesus like the Pharisees did, you are rejecting the invitation to the great heavenly banquet, for trusting in Jesus is the only way to get into the eternal banquet.

Jesus taught, "I am the way, and the truth, and the life. No one comes to the Father except through me" (John 14:6). The Pharisees gathered at the dinner rejected his teaching and did not believe.

They are the men in the parable who make excuses not to come to the banquet.

Talk about It

▶ Do you think the man who made the comment about the heavenly feast, believed in Jesus in the end? *(Parents, there is no correct answer to this question. Draw your children out to set up the next question.)*

▶ What about us, what do we need to do to accept Jesus's invitation to the great banquet? *(We must turn from our sin and trust in Jesus. Those who turn from their sin and place their trust in Jesus's death on the cross will join Jesus for that heavenly feast.)*

▶ Why did the Pharisees refuse to believe? *(Like the men who gave the excuses in the parable, they were more interested in earthly things—their power, position and the wealth it brought to them. They didn't realize that our sin makes all of us weak and helpless no matter how much we think we have.)*

Pray about It

Ask God to help everyone in your family believe in Jesus and not reject him.

Going Deeper

The excuses the men in the parable offer are weak. For example, a person purchasing a field would examine the property before purchasing it, not after. There is no need to go back to look at the field after it belongs to you, except to admire your purchase. The same is true of oxen. There is no need to check out your oxen after the sale. Furthermore, a new marriage is not an acceptable reason to decline an invitation to an important banquet.

The Pharisees refused Jesus's invitation. So Jesus turned to the uneducated fisherman, the sick, the poor, and the outcasts. Most of the Jews refused the invitation. So Jesus turned to the Samaritans, the Gentiles, and the tax collectors. They represent the poor, crippled, blind, and lame from the parable. The last line of the parable speaks a stinging rebuke to the Pharisees who refused to believe. "None of those men who were invited shall taste my banquet." We can only wonder if the man who assumed he would one day enjoy the heavenly feast understood what Jesus taught, and turned from his sin to believe.

The Pharisees would have known the writings of the prophet Isaiah, who foretold of a day when God would hold a great salvation banquet and invite all the peoples of the earth to feast (Isaiah 25:6–9). Isaiah said that God would swallow up death forever and wipe away tears from the faces of everyone invited. The Pharisees were so upset with Jesus that they missed connecting this prophecy to the parable.

Day Five

Listen Up

Read Luke 14:25–33:

> *Now great crowds accompanied him, and he turned and said to them, "If anyone comes to me and does not hate his own father and mother and wife and children and brothers and sisters, yes, and even his own life, he cannot be my disciple. Whoever does not bear his own cross and come after me cannot be my disciple. For which of you,*

desiring to build a tower, does not first sit down and count the cost, whether he has enough to complete it? Otherwise, when he has laid a foundation and is not able to finish, all who see it begin to mock him, saying, 'This man began to build and was not able to finish.' Or what king, going out to encounter another king in war, will not sit down first and deliberate whether he is able with ten thousand to meet him who comes against him with twenty thousand? And if not, while the other is yet a great way off, he sends a delegation and asks for terms of peace. So therefore, any one of you who does not renounce all that he has cannot be my disciple.

Think about It

After the banquet with the Pharisees, Luke told the story of a great crowd following Jesus along the way. As Jesus walked, he taught the people using three word pictures. First, he mentioned the picture of a person turning against his own family; second, a person building a tower; and finally, a king going off to war. The message of these word pictures is clear. If you want to be a disciple of Jesus, you must count the cost of following him. If you want to be a disciple of Jesus, you must believe in him.

At first, it can appear as if Jesus is going against the Bible's command to honor your father and mother. But Jesus is not teaching that Christians should hate their parents. Instead, he is encouraging believers to love God above every other relationship. A better way to understand this idea is to imagine what Andrew and Simon Peter's parents must have said when they found out the two brothers abandoned their fishing business to follow Jesus. While the Bible doesn't record their response, it is logical to assume they would have corrected their sons. Imagine them saying something like this: "Are you two so foolish? You can't just give up working to follow a roaming teacher."

What if Andrew and Simon's parents did command their sons to return to their nets and stop following Jesus? Should Simon Peter and Andrew obey their parents or obey Jesus who said, "Follow me, and I will make you fishers of men" (Matthew 4:19)?

We know the two fishermen followed Jesus over any objections their parents may have made. In this way, they may have disrespected their parents. When Jesus used the word *hate* he was using exaggerated language to make a point, that nothing, not even respecting our parents should stop us from following him and believing in Jesus. Sometimes following Jesus can cost us our friendships and in some countries, even your life. So, before you commit to following Jesus, count the cost—Jesus wants your whole life.

Talk about It

▶ What do people where you live need to give up to follow Jesus? *(Parents, for most of us, we only need to give up our sin. We must love God more than the approval of others, and live to honor him over what our friends say and do.)*

▶ What did Jesus mean by saying that you need to hate your parents in order to become a disciple? *(Jesus wasn't saying everyone who follows him should hate their parents. Jesus loved his mother Mary. What he was saying is that if it comes down to a choice—obey your parents who forbid you to follow Jesus, or follow Jesus, you must choose Jesus.)*

▶ What does it mean to carry your cross? *(The cross represents suffering. God will call each of us to suffer for our faith. At minimum, this entails rejecting the pleasures of the world. Instead of cheating, we must suffer long hours of hard work to learn. Instead of stealing to get rich quick, we suffer the long hours of labor to earn our money. But we do it all for the glory of God. Beyond living for God, our friends may make fun of us. Still we must pick up that cross and follow Jesus. But for some, the cross might involve imprisonment, rejection by their family, or even death.)*

Pray about It

Pray for the people in the world that are rejected by their families and persecuted for following Jesus. Then ask Jesus to help you count the cost of following him with your life.

Going Deeper

For most of us today, the cost of following Jesus in a Christian culture is minimal. But in many non-Christian cultures, a person who becomes a Christian is often cut off from his or her family. In some cases, they may be imprisoned or even killed for following Jesus. For those people, following Jesus means rejecting the false religion of your family. The rest of the family translates this as hatred and abandonment of their spiritual traditions and way of life.

In the western world we tend to think that the rest of the world practices its faith without the threat of persecution. But that's not true. To better acquaint yourself with the suffering of Christians around the world, consider reading a few stories from the book, *Persecuted, The Global Assault on Christians* by Paul Marshal, Lela Gilbert, and Nina Shea. To better acquaint your children, consider sharing a ministry to children provided by Voice of the Martyrs, www.kidsofcourage.com.

Week 10

The Lost Sheep, Lost Coin, and Lost Son

Let's Look at the Week. . .

This week we will spend our time reading Luke chapter 15, studying the parables of the Lost Sheep, the Lost Coin, and the Prodigal Son. These three parables paint a picture of God's love for his people and his eager desire to seek, find and restore his lost children to his family.

The lost and found theme we see in each of these parables shows up first in the Old Testament. Isaiah compared sinners to lost sheep, "All we like sheep have gone astray; we have turned—every one—to his own way; and the LORD has laid on him the iniquity of us all" (Isaiah 53:6). Jeremiah described how the leaders of Israel led the people astray saying, "My people have been lost sheep. Their shepherds have led them astray, turning them away on the mountains" (Jeremiah 50:6). The writer of Psalm 119:176 says, "I have gone astray like a lost sheep, seek your servant, for I do not forget your commandments."

In addition to these Old Testament passages, people across the globe are familiar with the famous John Newton hymn, "Amazing Grace." In it we sing:

> Amazing Grace, how sweet
> the sound,
> That saved a wretch like me.
> I once was lost, but now I'm
> found;
> Was blind, but now I see.

Get Ready

The action word of the week is repent.

The word *repent* means to turn around. It is used in the Bible to describe a person who was running from God but returned to follow him. Repentance also means turning from sin and turning toward God. If a thief repents, he stops stealing. When a liar repents, he seeks to tell the truth.

The Bible tells us that we must do two things to go to heaven. First, we must repent, or turn away from our sin. Secondly we must believe and turn to Jesus to be forgiven. We call the whole process of turning from our sin and turning toward Jesus, repentance.

This week we will learn that all of heaven rejoices when even a single person repents of their sin and turns to follow Jesus. We are all called to repentance and a deeper trust in Jesus.

Find the Lost Coin

(The goal of this activity is to give your children a fun opportunity to connect with the seek and find aspect of our lesson.)

Supplies:

- ▶ Two coins for each child playing (quarters work well as they are larger and easier to find)
- ▶ Bible opened up to Luke 19:10

Hide the coins in the room. Then inform your children that you have hidden coins for them to find. Explain that there are enough coins for each child to find two. Once they find their first coin they must come to the Bible and read aloud Luke 19:10, "For the Son of Man came to seek and to save the lost." (If your children are too young to read, they can tap you on the shoulder and have you read the verse.) After you or your child read the verse, that child may go to find a second coin. Read the verse again each time someone finds a coin. Encourage your children to express joy over the lost coins now found. Take the opportunity to point out that we are also lost in our sin, and that God rejoices every time one of his children is saved.

The repetition will emphasize this week's theme, which is the underlying truth behind the lost coin and lost sheep parables.

Day One

Listen Up

Read Luke 15:1–7:

> *Now the tax collectors and sinners were all drawing near to hear him. And the Pharisees and the scribes grumbled, saying, "This man receives sinners and eats with them."*
>
> *So he told them this parable: "What man of you, having a hundred sheep, if he has lost one of them, does not leave the ninety-nine in the open country, and go*

after the one that is lost, until he finds it? And when he has found it, he lays it on his shoulders, rejoicing. And when he comes home, he calls together his friends and his neighbors, saying to them, 'Rejoice with me, for I have found my sheep that was lost.' Just so, I tell you, there will be more joy in heaven over one sinner who repents than over ninety-nine righteous persons who need no repentance.

Think about It

Shepherds know their sheep so well that they can identify each one—even if they have a hundred! Because of this, they can mingle their sheep with another shepherd's. Once the two shepherds part ways, they each call their sheep by name, and the sheep follow. Occasionally one of their sheep might remain behind in another flock. In that case, they immediately recognize which specific sheep is missing. Throughout the day a shepherd looks to see that he has all of his sheep. Should he discover that one of his sheep is missing, he would leave the flock at once in search of the one that is lost.

Jesus used this picture of a shepherd searching for a lost sheep to teach a group of tax collectors and sinners about God's love for his lost children. Even as he taught the parable, Jesus was acting as a good shepherd, in search of lost sheep.

A few chapters later in Luke's gospel, we see Jesus, the Good Shepherd, find one of God's lost sheep and bring him home. It took place as Jesus traveled through Jericho on his way to Jerusalem. As Jesus pushed through the crowd, he noticed a man perched in a tree. Jesus walked up to a tree and called the man by name. "Zacchaeus, hurry and come down, for I must stay at your house today" (Luke 19:5). Zacchaeus, who was a tax collector, climbed down out of the tree with great joy. After meeting with Jesus, Zacchaeus repented of his greed and dishonesty and promised to repay everyone he cheated. In seeing this, Jesus exclaimed, "Today salvation has come to this house, since he also is a son of Abraham. For the Son of

Man came to seek and to save the lost" (Luke 19:9–10). Jesus went after Zacchaeus and called this lost sheep of God by name. He then brought him home back into the flock of God.

Talk about It

▶ Who do the shepherd and sheep represent in the parable? *(Jesus is the shepherd in the parable and the sheep represent sinners like you, lost in sin and not yet trusting Jesus as your shepherd.)*

▶ Jesus said, "There will be more joy in heaven over one sinner who repents." What does it mean to repent? Think of the story of Zacchaeus and how his life changed after meeting Jesus. *(To repent means to turn around—to stop running toward sin and instead, turn toward God. As a tax collector, Zacchaeus cheated the people. Once he met Jesus, he changed and agreed to give back the money he took from the people.)*

▶ The lost sheep in the parable do not go looking for the shepherd. Instead, the shepherd goes looking for them. How does God go looking for us? *(God uses the Bible, his Word, to call us just as a shepherd would call out on a hillside to his lost sheep. As the Word of God is proclaimed to us, the Holy Spirit opens our eyes to see and our ears to hear so we can believe. The Spirit of God gives us new life so that we can respond with joy to the call of the gospel.)*

Pray about It

We all begin life as lost sheep in need of Jesus. Ask God to come running after you and touch your life like he did that of Zacchaeus.

Going Deeper

Like in the Parable of the Lost Sheep, God is still searching for lost sheep today. Every Christian begins his life as one of God's lost sheep, eventually rescued through the ministry of Jesus Christ. Jesus is the Good Shepherd. He always finds the lost sheep. John records Jesus saying, "All that the Father gives me will come to me . . . I shall lose nothing of all that he has given me" (John 6:37 and 39). As the Good Shepherd, Jesus laid down his life for the sheep, by dying on the cross for our sin. Today, Jesus calls each of his lost sheep to come home. The call of Christ as the Good Shepherd sounds whenever we read, "Come to me, all who labor and are heavy laden, and I will give you rest. Take my yoke upon you, and learn from me, for I am gentle and lowly in heart, and you will find rest for your souls. For my yoke is easy, and my burden is light" (Matthew 11:28–30). When we read the words of Jesus to the young rich man, "Come, follow me" (Matthew 19:21), the same call comes to us. And just like in Jesus's day, whenever anyone turns away from his or her sin to trust in Jesus, all of heaven celebrates.

Day Two

Listen Up

Read Luke 15:8–10:

> *"Or what woman, having ten silver coins, if she loses one coin, does not light a lamp and sweep the house and seek diligently until she finds it? And when she has found it, she calls together her friends and neighbors, saying, 'Rejoice with me, for I have found the coin that I had lost.' Just so, I tell you, there is joy before the angels of God over one sinner who repents."*

Think about It

Did you ever lose something important and go on a house-wide search to find it? Perhaps you lost a book. First you would check all the places you normally keep your books like your backpack, desk, bookshelf, or table. But if you don't find it there, you start looking everywhere, even places that you know you would never put a book, like in your dresser, under your bed, and even in the dirty clothes' basket. If you can remember a time when you went frantically looking for something you lost, you know what the woman in the parable experienced. She lost a valuable coin and searched everywhere until she found it.

Now here is the truth God wants us to know about this parable: We are the lost coin, and God is like the woman searching to bring us back. We are lost because of sin—that separates us from God. We are found when the Holy Spirit opens our eyes to see our sin, repent of it, and follow Jesus. That's when we go from being lost to being found.

Whenever Jesus repeats something in his teaching, you can be sure it is important. So when Jesus ends the second parable with the same phrase, "There is joy before the angels of God over one sinner who repents," we are meant to take notice. Yesterday we learned that Jesus came to seek and save the lost. Jesus is a rescuer, who is saving God's children from the curse of sin and the control of Satan. Whenever he brings another lost sheep back into the flock, all of heaven explodes with thanks and praise, much like the crowd at a football stadium erupts when their team scores a touchdown.

Like the woman who won't stop searching till she finds her coin, God will seek and find all his lost children. God seeks after each one of his children with the same determination we have in searching for something important we lost—and he continues until we are found.

Talk about It

▶ In telling the Parable of the Lost Coin, what does Jesus repeat from the Parable of the Lost Sheep? How are the two parables similar? *(Jesus repeated that the angels in heaven rejoice when a sinner repents and joins the family of God. In general, both parables speak of losing something and searching until you find it.)*

▶ Who does the woman searching for the lost coin represent? *(The woman who is searching for the lost coin is a picture of Jesus seeking to save the lost children of God.)*

▶ Do you think that everyone listening to Jesus tell this parable repented of their sin and believed in Jesus? *(While the Bible doesn't tell us which people in the crowd believed and which did not, we know that not everyone believes. One of the ways you know you are a child of God is if you recognize the call of Jesus and follow him. Only his sheep [children] recognize his voice through the call of the Bible. Not everyone will be saved. Some refuse to believe until the day that they die. That's why it is so important to turn from your sin and trust in Jesus. Only God's children will do that.)*

Pray about It

Thank God for the way he searches for each one of his lost children like a woman who keeps searching until she finds her lost coin. Pray that God gives you the grace to turn away from your sin and trust in him.

Going Deeper

Isn't it a good thing to know that God is going to keep searching until he finds and restores each one of his children into his family? If a woman who lost a coin keeps searching until she finds it, how much harder will God work to find each of us lost children? Still, many of the Pharisees listening to Jesus missed the call. Satan blinded their eyes and they refused to believe and trust Jesus.

The apostle Paul explained Satan's work this way, "the god of this world has blinded the minds of the unbelievers, to keep them from seeing the light of the gospel of the glory of Christ" (2 Corinthians 4:4). Satan spreads lies like, "God wants to steal your joy and make you live by strict rules," or "God didn't create the universe; it came together by chance." Ultimately he tries to get you to believe that there is no God.

Jesus came into this lost world and is committed to winning back the children of God from the hold of the Satan. All of heaven is watching. Each time Jesus rescues one of God's children, all of heaven shouts for joy.

Day Three

Listen Up

Read Luke 15:11–19:

> *And he said, "There was a man who had two sons. And the younger of them said to his father, 'Father, give me the share of property that is coming to me.' And he divided his property between them. Not many days later, the younger son gathered all he had and took a journey into a far country, and there he squandered his property in reckless living. And when he had spent everything, a severe famine arose in that country, and he began to be in need. So he went and hired himself out to one of the citizens of that country, who sent him into his fields to feed pigs. And he was longing to be fed with the pods that the pigs ate, and no one gave him anything. But when he came to himself, he said, 'How many of my father's hired servants have more than enough bread, but I perish here with hunger! I will arise and go to my father, and I will say to him, "Father, I have sinned against heaven and before you. I am no longer worthy to be called your son. Treat me as one of your hired servants."'"*

Think about It

After sharing the Parable of the Lost Sheep and the Parable of the Lost Coin, Jesus told one of the most famous of all the parables, the Parable of the Prodigal Son. There are three main characters in this parable (the younger brother, the father, and the older brother). We will review them one at a time, starting with the younger son. As you study this parable, keep in mind the lost and found parables that came before it. The younger son is like the sheep who wandered away and the coin that the woman lost.

The younger son didn't like living under his father's rules. Sometimes we can be like that. Have your parents ever made a rule that you wished you didn't have to follow? Bedtime rules can be like that. You might think, if I lived on my own I could go to bed whenever I wanted. If I lived alone I could eat as much sugary cereal or as much candy as I wanted. As kids get older they can struggle with house rules more and more. Even though house rules are meant to help us, sinful pride can fool us into thinking that these rules are too strict.

Like the younger son in the parable, we are tempted to think we would be better off on our own, taking care of ourselves. It is not uncommon for children to see the authority of their parents as too strict. We can also think that God's rules in the Bible are designed to limit our fun. But that's not true; God gave us rules and parents to protect us from the foolish mistakes the younger son made. In the parable, the younger son disliked his father's rules so much that he ran away.

The consequences the younger son experienced after running away and squandering his inheritance should serve as a warning to us. After he ate with the pigs, his father's rule and authority didn't look so bad after all. In the end, God used the painful consequences of sin to bring the young son to his senses and help him repent (turn away) from his sinful rebellion. If we are wise, we can learn from his mistakes, so that we don't have to experience the same bad consequences.

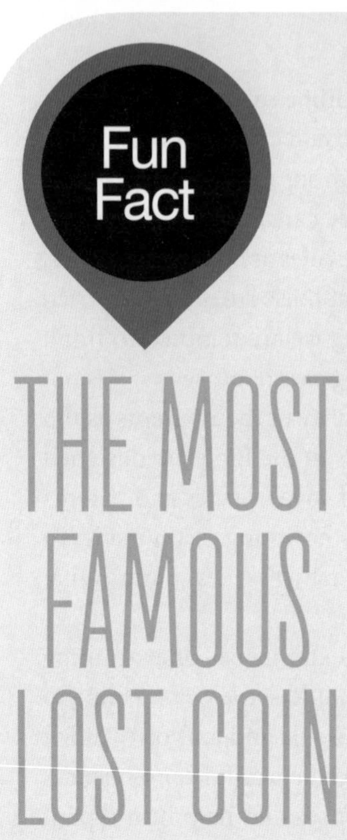

Jesus liked to tell stories using the common occurrences of everyday life. If he were alive and preaching in our time, he might have told the Parable of the Lost Car Key. We can all relate to losing something important. Although this particular lost coin is a component of a parable, it is the most well-known lost coin in our world.

Here is an interesting story of another famous lost coin. One of the rarest coins in the United States is the 1933 $20 Double Eagle gold piece. After the coins had been minted, before they went into circulation to be used by people to buy things, President Roosevelt made owning gold coins illegal. Before the coins could be melted down, one US Mint worker smuggled out a handful.

In 1944, the Secret Service discovered the theft and began a worldwide search for the lost coins. Just before they commenced their search, King Farouk of Egypt acquired one of the lost Double Eagles and applied for permission to own it. The US government agreed, and ownership of the coins was made legal. But in 1952, after the king died, his coin went missing again until 2002 when a coin dealer put up the lost coin for sale by auction. This famous rare lost coin fetched the incredible price of $7.6 million!

Talk about It

▶ Why do you think the younger son asked for his share of the money and left home? *(Parents, draw out your children here. There is no wrong answer.)*

▶ Can you remember a time when you thought a rule was too hard? *(Parents, you may be able to help your children think of a rule that they chafe under. Even something as simple as brushing their teeth before bed—or not eating too much candy, can illuminate this concept. Sure there is pleasure in eating a ton of candy or avoiding the work of brushing of teeth. But, the cost of having tooth decay well illustrates the foolishness of disregarding the rules.)*

▶ How was God at work in the life of the younger son? *(God did not allow the younger son to prosper. He lost all his money and ended up with the pigs, wishing he could eat their food, he was so hungry. Often God allows trials to come into our lives to help us to see our foolishness and our need for him.)*

Pray about It

Ask God to help you see the benefit of God's commandments and your parent's rules so that you can avoid the foolishness of the younger son.

Going Deeper

Normally, an inheritance is given to the son after the father dies. The younger son's request for his share of the inheritance was an insult to his father. It was as though he was saying, "Dad, I can't wait for you to die, just give my money now." He clearly disliked living at home, under his father's authority. But this arrogant young man soon discovered that it wasn't so easy to live on your own.

The son thought that if he left, he would be free of his father's rules, oversight, and could do what he wanted. But he didn't realize how his father's rules protected him and how good his life was back home. Soon his money was gone, and he found himself with the pigs. It is there, longing to satisfy his hunger with the scraps thrown for the pigs, that the younger son realized how foolish and sinful he had become.

Sin lies to us. It promises freedom and happiness, but in the end it leads us to sorrow. The Apostle Paul said it like this, "the one who sows to please his sinful nature, from that nature will reap destruction" (Galatians 6:8 NIV).

Day Four

Listen Up

Read Luke 15:20–24:

> *And he arose and came to his father. But while he was still a long way off, his father saw him and felt compassion, and ran and embraced him and kissed him. And the son said to him, 'Father, I have sinned against heaven and before you. I am no longer worthy to be called your son.' But the father said to his servants, 'Bring quickly the best robe, and put it on him, and put a ring on his hand, and shoes on his feet. And bring the fattened calf and kill it, and let us eat and celebrate. For this my son was dead, and is alive again; he was lost, and is found.' And they began to celebrate.*

Think about It

At this point in the story, most people would expect the father to be furious with his foolish son. But what we see unfold in the story is completely different. The father is excited to see his son return and ran with joy to embrace him. Back in Jesus's day, older men did not run in public. It was considered undignified for an older man to do so. Yet when the father saw his son, he didn't care what people thought, he ran to welcome his son. Another interesting fact is that the father was the first one to spot his son. He spotted him while he was still far off. It makes you wonder if the father kept an eye out, always looking for his son, believing he would one day return home.

Now it is one thing for the son's dad to welcome him back. What is even more surprising is the father's call to hold a feast and give gifts to celebrate the son's return. The father's joyful response is similar to the heavenly celebration Jesus references in the two previous parables. Do you remember? He said, "there will be more joy in heaven over one sinner who repents" (Luke 15:7).

The younger son in the parable represents all of us who have turned away from God in our sin. God is like the father who runs to welcome his son home. When we repent from our sinful, rebellious pride, God cancels our debt and joyfully welcomes us back into his family. We become brothers and sisters of Jesus and receive gifts—an inheritance we do not deserve that God is keeping for us (1 Peter 1:4).

Talk about It

▶ How did the son expect his father to react? *(The son expected his father would not be happy. That's why he came ready to take a position as a servant rather than a son.)*

▶ Why is the father's reaction toward his returning son surprising? What did you think his reaction would be? *(Parents, draw out your children. It is too easy to jump on the bandwagon and say you knew the son's father would have a forgiving welcome and celebration. The truth is we would all expect the father to scold his son.)*

▶ How does this parable relate to us? *(Every one of us is like the younger son who turned away from God to a life of sin. When God opens our eyes to understand that we are sinners who need to return to the Father, we, like the younger brother, turn from our sinful ways and run back to God.)*

Pray about It

Ask God to help each person in your family recognize the loving way God our Father desires to welcome us back home, into the household of God.

Going Deeper

Like the father who ran to meet his son, God takes the initiative to rescue us. John 3:16–17 states, "For God so loved the world, that he gave his only Son, that whoever believes in him should not perish but have eternal life. For God did not send his Son into the world to condemn the world, but in order that the world might be saved through him." God took the initiative to send his Son Jesus to die on the cross to provide a way for us to be forgiven and welcomed home.

In addition, God controls the circumstances of our lives to bring the perfect trial that will lead us to repentance (Romans 8:28). God sends his Spirit to convict us of sin (John 16:8) so that we understand our need for Christ.

Day Five

Listen Up

Read Luke 15:25–32:

> *"Now his older son was in the field, and as he came and drew near to the house, he heard music and dancing. And he called one of the servants and asked what these things meant. And he said to him, 'Your brother has come, and your father has killed the fattened calf, because he has received him back safe and sound.' But he was angry and refused to go in. His father came out and entreated him, but he answered his father, 'Look, these many years I have served you, and I never disobeyed your command, yet you never gave me a young goat, that I might celebrate with my friends. But when this son of yours came, who has devoured your property with prostitutes, you killed the fattened calf for him!' And he said to him, 'Son, you are always with me, and all that is mine is yours. It was fitting to celebrate and be glad, for this your brother was dead, and is alive; he was lost, and is found.'"*

Think about It

Most people refer to the parable we've been studying as the Parable of the Prodigal Son, naming the parable after the younger son who ran away. Often they miss that the second half is the most important part of the parable. While there are lessons to be learned from the younger son, the main reason Jesus told the parable was to describe the reaction of the older brother. The older brother didn't want his father to forgive the younger son. He thought he should be punished for his sin.

Do you agree with the older brother? Was the father wrong to celebrate the younger brother's return? Of course, we know from the story that it was good for the father to forgive his son. But forgiving people is not easy. Often our sinful pride wants them to have to pay for what they did, and we would rather not forgive them.

The older brother looked down at his younger brother. It was one thing to welcome him home, but he thought the celebration was not fair. It was true that the older brother didn't run away and squander money like his younger brother did, but the older brother was just as selfish. He was only thinking about himself. He also wanted a robe and a ring. He was jealous of his brother; his dad never gave him a party like that. So you see, instead of rejoicing with his father in the repentance of his younger brother's return, the older brother ran away in his heart and rebelled by refusing to join the celebration. In the end, he sinned much like his brother. They younger brother rejected his father's rule and ran away. The older brother became bitter and jealous and so rejected his father's rule and refused to attend the party. The older brother's sin might not look so bad at first, but once you see that he is disobeying his father and withholding forgiveness toward his younger brother, you realize that his sin is just as serious.

Talk about It

▶ How would you describe the reaction of the older brother to his younger brother's return? *(Parents, allow your children to describe his actions in their own words, but steer them toward words such as* prideful *and* self-righteous*—the older brother thought he was better than his younger brother.)*

▶ How is the response of the older brother similar to the way the Pharisees treated Jesus? *(The Pharisees did not welcome or celebrate repentant sinners who flocked to hear Jesus's teachings. They were jealous of Jesus's popularity and were proud, just like the older brother in the parable.)*

▶ Do people still struggle with self-righteousness today? Can you think of a few examples? *(Yes, we still struggle with self-righteousness today. Like the Pharisees, we read the words of Jesus in the Bible and too often think they apply to others rather than ourselves. We look down on those struggling with sin, thinking we are better than they are. We also boast in our accomplishments.)*

Pray about It

Ask God to help each person in your family see they are a sinner who needs to run to Jesus for grace and forgiveness.

Going Deeper

Jesus details the objections of the older brother as a way to rebuke the self-righteous Pharisees who criticized Jesus saying, "this man receives sinners and eats with them" (Luke 15:2).

Instead of celebrating the repentance of the tax collectors, who came to listen to Jesus, the Pharisees complained. They of all people, who looked down on the tax collectors should have rejoiced that these men were interested in learning about God from Jesus. Instead, they criticized Jesus for welcoming them. At least the tax collectors were aware of their sin and their need for Jesus's teaching. Most of the religious rulers thought they didn't need Jesus. They got angry when they saw Jesus reach out to sinners and offer them forgiveness—just like the older brother in the parable became angry when his father celebrated his brother's return.

While the Pharisees worked hard to keep the Law on the outside, their hearts were sinful. Like the older brother in the parable, the Pharisees looked down upon sinners and did not rejoice when they flocked to Jesus to hear his teaching.

At the end of the parable, the father seeks after the older son and pleads with him to join in the celebration. Still, the son refuses to give up his self-righteous bitterness toward his younger brother and his anger against his father for welcoming him home. In a similar way, the Pharisees rejected the appeals of Jesus and refused to follow him. That led them to commit a far more serious sin than any of the tax collectors; they sent Jesus to the cross to die.

Week 11

Heaven and Hell

Let's Look at the Week. . .

As Jesus drew closer to Jerusalem, his teaching became more serious. The parables he used spoke of heaven and hell and a final judgment. The nearer he got to his death, the graver his words to the religious rulers became. Today these same parables call us to repent and believe in Jesus or face God's judgment for our sin. These are serious topics for children to study—and some might suggest we wait till kids are older to talk about them. But parents regularly purchase Bibles for their children as soon as they are able to read and encourage them to read through the gospels. So taking a closer look to study some of the more challenging topics, like heaven and hell, is important.

One of the scariest of the parables is the Parable of The Rich Man and Lazarus. The story is of two men who lived on earth and died. One man goes to heaven, the other to hell. Through the parable we see that once we die, it is too late to turn from our sin and believe in Jesus. The men he spoke to thought all you needed was to be born into the family of Abraham, not believe in Jesus.

Get Ready

The action word of the week is believe.

Believe is a word we use to describe something we know to be true. It is easy to believe in things we can prove with our five senses. We believe the sky is blue because we can see it with our eyes. We believe that rabbits have soft fur because we can touch them with our hands.

But there are other things that we believe and know to be true that cannot be proven with our five senses. For example, we believe Abraham Lincoln was the sixteenth president of the United States even though we can't see him—he died more than one hundred years ago. The reason we believe this is because we place our trust and faith in the history books that say he was our president. We trust the testimony of people who did see him. We believe the historical accounts of Jesus that are found in the gospels. We can't see Jesus today, but we put our trust in the witnesses who did see him. For example, more than 500 people saw Jesus alive after he rose again from the grave.

Sometimes we must believe something by faith—without seeing anything at all. We believe in God the Father by faith. We can't see God the Father and no one (except for Jesus) has ever seen God the Father. But if we believe in Jesus and all that he taught, we can trust that his teachings are true.

This week we will study the parables from Luke 16 that prompt us to ask ourselves, who or what are we trusting in for our help and salvation?

Bubbles Through the Hoop

(The goal of this activity is to recognize we are all running from God, but he is seeking us.)

Supplies:

- Hula hoop (You can also use a laundry basket and have the children try to blow bubbles into the basket.)
- Jar of Bubbles

Tell your children that you are going to play a game called bubbles through the hoop. The object of the game is to see if you can blow a bubble through the hoop before it pops. (Parents, you can hold the hoop three feet from the starting line.)

First, blow a wand full of bubbles into the air, then try to blow the bubbles with puffs of air from your mouth to carry them through the hoop (or into the laundry basket) your parent is holding. Once you get a bubble through the hoop, or if all the bubbles pop, your turn is complete.

After your children are successful by moving a bubble through the hoop, tell them to turn away from the hoop and blow their bubbles in the opposite direction. As soon as they create the bubbles, move your hula hoop over to the bubbles and try to get as many to pass through the hoop as you can. (The object is to show how many more bubbles you can pass through the hoop when you

Day One

Listen Up

Read Luke 16:1–9:

> *He also said to the disciples, "There was a rich man who had a manager, and charges were brought to him that this man was wasting his possessions. And he called him and said to him, 'What is this that I hear about you? Turn in the account of your management, for you can no longer be manager.' And the manager said to himself, 'What shall I do, since my master is taking the management away from me? I am not strong enough to dig, and I am*

are moving the hoop toward the bubbles instead of blowing the bubbles toward the hoop.)

Then offer your children this explanation. The bubbles are like people on the earth. The hoop is the door to heaven that God is holding open. We tend to think life is like the first phase of the game where we have to try to get to heaven by our work (blowing our bubble through the hoop). But in reality, we are all running away from heaven, and God is seeking after us. That's like God moving the hula hoop (the way to heaven) over to our bubble. Remember the lost sheep? God comes after us.

But here is the serious part of the exercise. The bubbles don't last forever—they all pop. Like the bubbles, we will not live forever. The Bible tells us that God has planned a time for each of us to die, and then to face judgment (Hebrews 9:27). On that day it will be too late to believe in Jesus. Those who do not trust in Jesus while they are alive will not join him in heaven after they die.

ashamed to beg. I have decided what to do, so that when I am removed from management, people may receive me into their houses.' So, summoning his master's debtors one by one, he said to the first, 'How much do you owe my master?' He said, 'A hundred measures of oil.' He said to him, 'Take your bill, and sit down quickly and write fifty.' Then he said to another, 'And how much do you owe?' He said, 'A hundred measures of wheat.' He said to him, 'Take your bill, and write eighty.' The master commended the dishonest manager for his shrewdness. For the sons of this world are more shrewd in dealing with their own generation than the sons of light. And I tell you, make friends for yourselves by means of unrighteous wealth, so that when it fails they may receive you into the eternal dwellings.

Think about It

When the manager in the parable learned he was going to lose his job, he instructed the borrowers to reduce their bills. While it seems like he was cheating his master, he was only cutting out the unlawful interest. Since the original practice was illegal, there was nothing the master could do, but praise the shrewdness of his manager.

Now we need to be careful what we draw from this parable. Jesus wasn't teaching his disciples that it was OK to cheat people as long as the paperwork looked good. Nor was he saying that it is OK to lie about a business deal. He was simply using a common lending practice to make an important point. If unbelievers know how to be shrewd with their money, the disciples—and all Christians after them should be shrewd with their money as well.

So how can we be shrewd with our money? In week eight we learned that Jesus taught the disciples not to store up for yourself treasure on earth, but store up for yourself treasure in heaven (Matthew 6:19–20). The shrewd Christian knows that we can invest our treasure in heaven by supporting God's kingdom today. If the unbelieving earthly manager was shrewd enough about money to think ahead, we too should think ahead and invest our money accordingly. If you invest your money in a bank, they give you interest (a little bit more money) that you can spend on earth. By reducing the merchants' bills, the manager increased his chances of securing another job. He invested in his future employment. In a similar way, sharing with those in need invests in our future reward in heaven.

Talk about It

▶ What did the manager do, once he realized he was going to lose his job? *(He reduced the merchants' debts in effort to regain their favor.)*

▶ Who do the people in this parable represent? Does anyone in the parable represent God? *(This is one of those parables where the characters in the parable do not represent God, they simply stand to illustrate a point.)*

▶ What is Jesus trying to teach us regarding money? *(We should be shrewd with our money. While we can't spend earthly riches after we die, we can store up treasure in heaven by using our money to bless others. If we invest our money on earth, we receive an earthly return, but by investing in kingdom work, we are investing in a heavenly return.)*

Pray about It

Pray that God would help you think of ways to bless others with your money and possessions so that you can store up for yourself treasure in heaven.

Going Deeper

To understand the Parable of the Dishonest Manager, you need to know how lending worked in Jesus's day. The law of Moses taught that it was wrong to charge your fellow Israelite interest (Deuteronomy 23:19). Interest is charging a person money to borrow money. So, to avoid breaking God's Law, wealthy men appointed managers to oversee their lending. These managers were shrewd men who knew how to get around the Law. And this is how they did it: if a fellow businessman needed to borrow fifty barrels of oil, but had no money to pay, the manager would propose a deal. He would give him the fifty barrels he needed, but write down that he took one hundred barrels, doubling his debt.

To an outsider reading the agreement, it would look as though the neighbor borrowed one hundred barrels and agreed to pay back one hundred barrels. This practice hid the fact that the manager was actually charging 100% interest on the deal; making the borrower pay double in return. Although this process looked good on paper, it was illegal and opposed the Law of God.

The most challenging line in the parable is, "make friends for yourselves by means of unrighteous wealth." Jesus isn't saying that we should cheat in effort to gain wealth and friends. The term *unrighteous wealth* refers to worldly riches and treasures. We should use our money and treasures to bless others. As we do so, we will simultaneously gain friends and heavenly treasure. Do you know of someone who is struggling to make ends meet? Consider blessing them through a financial gift. You will bless the friendship and store up heavenly treasure.

Day Two

Listen Up

Read Luke 16:10–15:

> *"One who is faithful in a very little is also faithful in much, and one who is dishonest in a very little is also dishonest in much. If then you have not been faithful in the unrighteous wealth, who will entrust to you the true*

riches? And if you have not been faithful in that which is another's, who will give you that which is your own? No servant can serve two masters, for either he will hate the one and love the other, or he will be devoted to the one and despise the other. You cannot serve God and money."

The Pharisees, who were lovers of money, heard all these things, and they ridiculed him. And he said to them, "You are those who justify yourselves before men, but God knows your hearts. For what is exalted among men is an abomination in the sight of God.

Think about It

After sharing the Parable of the Shrewd Manager, Jesus summed up his teaching with this truth: "You cannot serve God and money." The word Jesus used for money is *mammon*, which includes both money and possessions—the things we own like our clothes, a bicycle or car, home, and furniture. The Pharisees who were listening ridiculed (mocked and criticized) Jesus for this teaching. They missed an opportunity to evaluate their own lives to see where they might love money more than God. While we don't know if they were rich, we do know they failed to love Jesus and apply his teaching to their lives.

Thousands of years later, today, we are reading Jesus's teaching and seeing the reaction of the Pharisees. But rather than judge these men, we should look at our own lives. The Bible passage asks us the same question—who do we love and serve with our riches—do we serve money as our god or do we serve God with our money? Do we live for God and invest in his kingdom, or do we live for the pleasures that money can bring? Are we generous with our mammon (money and possessions) or do we neglect to give to the mission of the church and God's people in need? Those are the kind of questions the Pharisees didn't want to ask.

Earthly riches distract us from the things of God. Instead of trusting God to meet a need, we think we need more money to buy it. Instead of longing to be with God in heaven, we long for more money. For some, just the thought of living for God instead of money is enough to keep them from believing and trusting in Jesus.

Talk about It

▶ What lesson was Jesus teaching about money? *(You cannot serve both God and money.)*

▶ How did the Pharisees respond to Jesus? *(The Pharisees mocked Jesus.)*

▶ Can you think of any ways to help a person know if they love mammon (their money and possessions) more than God? *(Parents, draw your children out regarding this question. One of the ways we know we love our money or possessions more than God is how we respond when we lose them. Use the example of a friend borrowing a toy and not returning it, or worse—breaking it. How we view our money and possessions is an indicator of what's taking place in our hearts. You might ask your children: how do you spend your allowance money? Do you share a portion with God's kingdom, or do you spend it on yourself? Are you generous and willing to share with those in need, or do you hoard it to yourself?)*

Pray about It

Ask God to help you love him most of all.

Going Deeper

As parents, it is essential to invite your children into this concept of biblical giving. Otherwise, they may miss a wonderful opportunity. When the Spirit convicts you to give generously, share this with your children. Allow them to learn from your example.

These passages should help us to evaluate how much we are giving. In our prosperous culture, it can be tempting to give a little bit to make us feel better, while at the same time, still finding our joy in all the money we have left over. Remember who Jesus praised for giving? Jesus said, "Truly, I say to you, this poor widow has put in more than all those who are contributing to the offering box. For they all contributed out of their abundance, but she out of her poverty has put in everything she had, all she had to live on" (Mark 12:43–44).

If going through this week's Scriptures convicts you regarding your level of giving, share this with your kids. Pray and ask God what you could give to invest in his kingdom. Then let your kids in on the gift you plan to give—call it a family gift. Ultimately, when we as parents give our money or possessions or both away, the whole family participates in the sacrifice and blessing.

Day Three

Listen Up

Read Luke 16:19–26:

> *"There was a rich man who was clothed in purple and fine linen and who feasted sumptuously every day. And at his gate was laid a poor man named Lazarus, covered with sores, who desired to be fed with what fell from the rich man's table. Moreover, even the dogs came and licked his sores. The poor man died and was carried by the angels to Abraham's side. The rich man also died and was buried, and in Hades, being in torment, he lifted up his eyes and saw Abraham far off and Lazarus at his side. And he called out, 'Father Abraham, have mercy on me, and send*

Lazarus to dip the end of his finger in water and cool my tongue, for I am in anguish in this flame.' But Abraham said, 'Child, remember that you in your lifetime received your good things, and Lazarus in like manner bad things; but now he is comforted here, and you are in anguish. And besides all this, between us and you a great chasm has been fixed, in order that those who would pass from here to you may not be able, and none may cross from there to us.'

Think about It

It may feel scary to imagine someone spending eternity in an inescapable place of fire. But we never have to worry about going there if we place our trust in Jesus.

Jesus delivered this parable to a group of Pharisees who loved money more than God and who refused to believe in Jesus—they ridiculed him (Luke 16:14). They enjoyed their lives on earth, unconcerned for the judgment awaiting them. They were not giving much thought to the consequences of their actions. The main point of the parable is to warn the Pharisees of the coming judgment. Normally Jesus doesn't give characters in the parables names, but here, the poor man is given a name—Lazarus, which helps us connect with the character in a unique and personal way.

The Jews were called "children of Abraham" and believed that they would go to join Abraham when they died. They believed all "good" Jews, who kept the Law, would go to heaven. This parable was meant to shake up their thinking.

The parable describes hell as a terrible place of suffering and fire, a place where the man longs for a drop of water. This description of hell is consistent with what Jesus taught elsewhere where he said it was a place of unquenchable fire (Mark 9:43).

Luke records this parable as a warning to all of us. If we turn away from Jesus and live for this life, we will one day go before God and be judged. But if we believe and trust in Jesus, on that day of judgment we will be welcomed by God and join Abraham and all the saints who put their trust in God's saving plan.

Talk about It

▶ What do we learn about hell (hades) from this parable? *(We learn that hades is a real place, of terrible suffering, that you cannot escape.)*

▶ How can a person get to heaven and avoid the fires of hell? *(There is only one way for us to get to heaven. We need to turn away from our sin and believe in Jesus.)*

▶ How can we relate the characters in this parable to people alive today? *(We live in a world of plenty. A lot of people reject Jesus and trust in their own riches. It would be easy for us to trust in our riches too.)*

Pray about It

Ask God to open the eyes of each person in your family to see their need for Jesus and believe in him.

Going Deeper

We will take two days to study the Parable of the Rich Man and Lazarus. As we think about this parable, it is important to remember that parables are stories, usually designed to teach a single truth. So we need to be careful not to use the stories by themselves to shape our theology. That's why it is important to know the context (who is Jesus teaching and what is happening in the passages surrounding the parable). Then we can compare what the rest of the Bible teaches about the same topics. So in this parable, Jesus isn't saying all rich men go to hell and all poor men who suffer illnesses go to heaven. We know from other parts of the Bible that we are saved by our faith, not by our works or suffering.

Consider these Scriptures that talk about our faith as the basis of our salvation:

> "For by grace you have been saved through faith. And this is not your own doing; it is the gift of God, not a result of works, so that no one may boast. For we are his workmanship, created in Christ Jesus for good works, which God prepared beforehand, that we should walk in them." (Ephesians 2:8–10)

> "We ourselves are Jews by birth and not Gentile sinners; yet we know that a person is not justified by works of the law but through faith in Jesus Christ, so we also have believed in Christ Jesus, in order to be justified by faith in Christ and not by works of the law, because by works of the law no one will be justified." (Galatians 2:15–16)

Day Four

Listen Up

Read Luke 16:27–31:

> *And he said, 'Then I beg you, father, to send him to my father's house—for I have five brothers—so that he may warn them, lest they also come into this place of torment.' But Abraham said, 'They have Moses and the Prophets; let*

them hear them.' And he said, 'No, father Abraham, but if someone goes to them from the dead, they will repent.' He said to him, 'If they do not hear Moses and the Prophets, neither will they be convinced if someone should rise from the dead.'"

Think about It

In this second half of the Parable of the Rich Man and Lazarus, the rich man begged father Abraham to send Lazarus back to earth to warn his brothers. Even if it is too late for him, he wanted his brothers to turn from their sin and believe. He didn't want them to suffer his same fate.

Abraham answered by saying the rich man's brothers already had Moses and the Prophets. By this he meant that they already had the Bible passages that pointed to Jesus and show that Jesus is the promised Messiah. For instance, the story of the Passover, where the Jews painted the blood of a lamb on their doorframe, pointed forward to Jesus, the Lamb of God who takes away our sin. Those who daubed the blood of a lamb upon their doorframes escaped God's judgment (Exodus 12:13), just like we who believe in Jesus and his death on the cross will escape God's judgment for our sin.

The final line of the parable, "neither will they be convinced if someone should rise from the dead," doesn't just refer to the idea of Lazarus returning from the grave to warn the rich man's brothers. Jesus is also talking about the way people would respond when he too would rise from the dead. Even after Jesus rose from the dead, the Pharisees still refused to believe.

Today, we have the testimony of Moses and the Prophets written down in the Bible for us to read. We know that Jesus rose from the dead. Still, millions of people refuse to believe and trust in Jesus. They will end up like the rich man, punished in the fires of hell for their sin, wishing they could warn their family that everything the Bible says about Jesus is true.

Talk about It

▶ Why does the rich man want Lazarus to go back home? *(He wants to send him back to warn his brothers.)*

▶ What do you think the rich man would say to his brothers if he could go back? *(Parents, this is an important question. His warning would be something like, "Turn away from your sins and believe in Jesus, he really is the Son of God who the Father sent to die on the cross for our sins. If you trust in Jesus, you will go to be with God, but if you do not believe, you will be sent to hell, which is a real place. Once you are there you can never leave." This is the same warning we are all to take from this parable.)*

▶ Why wasn't Lazarus allowed to go back? *(Lazarus was not allowed to go back because his brothers would refuse to believe, even if they saw a man who came back from the dead. We see the same refusal to believe today. Even though Jesus rose from the dead, upholding the accuracy of his Word, people still refuse to believe.)*

Pray about It

Ask God to open the eyes of each person in your family to believe so every one of them might end up like Lazarus, with God in heaven.

Going Deeper

Jesus said the rich man and his family had the Prophets but still did not believe. Likewise, many of the Jews rejected Jesus's fulfillment of prophecies.

The Prophets foretold that a far-off son of David would be born of a virgin (Isaiah 7:14) in Bethlehem (Micah 5:2) to deliver God's people. He would reign on David's throne as king (Jeremiah 23:5), would give sight to the blind, and set the prisoner free (Isaiah 42:7). The promised Messiah would take the sins of the people upon himself and take their punishment (Isaiah 53:5). Early in his ministry, Jesus said his ministry fulfilled these prophecies, but most of the Pharisees and other religious rulers refused to believe.

The rich man's appeal to send Lazarus back is logical. No one could argue against a man back from the dead! So, how could Jesus be so certain that his brothers would not believe?

Think about it for a moment. Think about the name Lazarus. Why do you think Jesus gave him that name? It is the very same name given to the man that Jesus called out of the tomb a short time later. Remember the story? Lazarus was dead for days and Jesus called out to him and said, "Lazarus come forth!" Immediately Lazarus came walking out of the tomb, back from the grave. Scores of people saw him. You can imagine what Lazarus might have said to those who doubted—"God is real, Jesus is real. He is the Messiah! All that the Prophets and Moses said about him is true. I was dead and went to Abraham's side but God sent me back to warn you. Please, I beg of you, put your trust in Jesus."

But, how did the Pharisees respond to the raising of Lazarus from the grave? They decided to put Jesus and Lazarus both to death (John 11:45–53, John 12:8–11). The Pharisees were given the same chance the rich man requested God give to his brothers, but they still refused to believe.

Listen Up

Read Matthew 20:1–16:

> *"For the kingdom of heaven is like a master of a house who went out early in the morning to hire laborers for his vineyard. After agreeing with the laborers for a denarius a day, he sent them into his vineyard. And going out about the third hour he saw others standing idle in the marketplace, and to them he said, 'You go into the vineyard too, and whatever is right I will give you.' So they went. Going out again about the sixth hour and the ninth hour, he did the same. And about the eleventh hour he went out and found others standing. And he said to them, 'Why do you stand here idle all day?' They said to him, 'Because no one has hired us.' He said to them, 'You go into the vineyard too.' And when evening came, the owner of the vineyard said to his foreman, 'Call the laborers and pay them their wages, beginning with the last, up to the first.' And when those hired about the eleventh hour came, each of them received a denarius. Now when those hired first came, they thought they would receive more, but each of them also received a denarius. And on receiving it they grumbled at the master of the house, saying, 'These last worked only one hour, and you have made them equal to us who have borne the burden of the day and the scorching heat.' But he replied to one of them, 'Friend, I am doing you no wrong. Did you not agree with me for a denarius? Take what belongs to you and go. I choose to give to this last worker as I give to you. Am I not allowed to do what I choose with what belongs to me? Or do you begrudge my generosity?' So the last will be first, and the first last."*

It takes three years from the time you plant your grapevines until you can harvest grapes. Each grapevine can produce 15 pounds of fruit, and an acre of grapevines will produce as much as 8,000 pounds, but a wise vinedresser will thin the grapes to reduce the total to below 6,000 pounds The less fruit on the vine, the better the quality of grape and the wine. Six thousand pounds of grapes will make around 2,500 bottles of wine.

While you only need one vinedresser to prune the vines, you need a team of laborers to gather the ripened grapes. When it comes time to harvest, the owner of a vineyard must hire enough workers to harvest and process the grapes quickly, particularly if he doesn't have the ability to keep the grapes cool. The vineyard owner must also deter the birds that are eager to snack upon the ripened grapes.

Think about It

We've learned that it is important when looking at a parable to consider its context. Context is all that's going on around the parable. Who was Jesus teaching? What other lessons did Jesus teach before or after the parable?

In this context, Jesus tells the Parable of the Workers in the Vineyard after an interaction with a young rich man. Jesus invited the rich man to sell all that he had, give to the poor, and then come and follow Jesus. Instead, the man walked away sad, for he had many possessions. The disciples questioned Jesus about how hard it was to get to heaven. In response, Jesus taught them this parable.

The message of the parable is a simple one—we don't get to heaven based on our work; we get to heaven based on God's grace. Even though Jesus asked the young rich man to give up his possessions, it was not that work which would earn him a place in heaven. The master in the parable pays everyone the same, even those who only worked the last portion of the day. Think of the thief on the cross. He lived a sinful life, right up to his last day, where he hung with Jesus on the cross. But he turned from his sin and called out to Jesus and believed. Jesus said to him, "today you will be with me in paradise" (Luke 23:43).

Talk about It

▶ In the Parable of the Workers in the Vineyard, the men hired at the end of the day got paid the same as those who worked the whole day. Why did they get paid the same? *(Even though the workers didn't deserve a whole day's pay, the master extended grace to them. Jesus used this story to help the disciples understand that we can't work our way into heaven; it is a gift of God's grace. While some may serve and follow God all their lives—perhaps they are born into a Christian family—others, like the thief on the cross, can still get to heaven at the end of their life. It is about God's call and his grace. The master called all of the workers in the parable to service. Apart from his call, they would not have found work.)*

▶ What is the one main point Jesus is trying to teach us through this parable? *(The main point of this parable is that we can't get to heaven by our works.)*

▶ If we can't work our way to heaven, how is it that we deserve to be welcomed into heaven since we are sinners who deserve to be punished? *(We get to heaven by trusting in Jesus's work. Jesus lived a perfect life in our place, and then died on the cross to take the punishment for our sin. When we give our lives to Jesus, we are investing in his work. If we trust in Jesus, God welcomes us for all eternity.)*

Pray about It

Take time to praise God for sending his Son Jesus to die and rise again so that we can be forgiven and raised to new life after death. Thank God that we don't have to earn our way to heaven, but that we come by his call and grace.

Going Deeper

While Matthew doesn't record an explanation for this parable, he does provide more information. Jesus goes on to give his disciples a prophetic glimpse of the next few days. Consider the following prediction of Jesus's death:

> And as Jesus was going up to Jerusalem, he took the twelve disciples aside, and on the way he said to them, "See, we are going up to Jerusalem. And the Son of Man will be delivered over to the chief priests and scribes, and they will condemn him to death and deliver him over to the Gentiles to be mocked and flogged and crucified, and he will be raised on the third day" (Matthew 20:17–19).

Jesus gave the following seven predictions about what was about to happen to him:

1. He would be delivered over to the chief priests.
2. The chief priests would condemn him to death.
3. The chief priests would deliver him over to the Gentiles.
4. Jesus would be mocked.
5. Jesus would be flogged.
6. Jesus would be crucified.
7. Jesus would rise from the dead on the third day.

Of course, all of these came true. Judas betrayed Jesus to the chief priests with a kiss, the chief priests held a rigged trial and condemned him to death, then delivered him over to the Romans. Along the way, Jesus was mocked, flogged, and crucified. Then, on the third day an angel from heaven came and rolled the stone away, and Jesus burst forth, rising from the grave in power.

Week 12

Everybody Needs Jesus

Let's Look at the Week. . .

Six days before his death on the cross (crucifixion), Jesus rode into Jerusalem on a donkey. The crowds lined the way, spread their cloaks on the ground and waved palm branches in the air. (That's why we celebrate Palm Sunday, after Jesus's entry into Jerusalem.) The people shouted, "Hosanna! Blessed is he who comes in the name of the Lord, even the King of Israel!" (John 12:13). The Pharisees who were watching, demanded Jesus correct the crowd saying, "Teacher, rebuke your disciples" (Luke 19:39). These religious leaders were jealous of Jesus's popularity. They did not believe that Jesus was the prophesied King, who would sit on the throne of David.

This week we'll look at the parables Jesus taught to the religious rulers in Jerusalem just a few days before his crucifixion. We will start our study with the Parable of the Pharisee and Tax Collector from Luke's gospel. In that parable, Jesus contrasts the self-righteousness of the Pharisee with the repentance of a tax collector. From there we will move on to other parables that address the unbelief of the religious rulers.

As we study these parables, which expose the self-righteousness and unbelief of the religious rulers, we should be careful to look at ourselves. It is easy to become critical of them and miss the opportunity to examine our own hearts. If we are wise, we can learn from what we read so that we don't repeat their same mistakes. This week's parables are meant to help us see that there is a little bit of Pharisee in us all.

Get Ready

The action word of the week is trust.

Trust is a word we use to say we believe in someone or something, and we are willing to put ourselves at risk as proof. It is one thing to say you believe a bridge is strong enough to drive a car across, but when you are the one driving the car over the bridge you trust the bridge with your life.

We trust doctors to give us the right medicine. We trust airplanes to fly us from city to city. As Christians, we trust Jesus to save us from our sin. But not everyone trusts in Jesus; some trust their good works to get them to heaven. In this week's parables be on the lookout for people who are trusting God.

Sticky Note Grab

(The object of this activity is to teach the concept of self-righteousness to your children.)

Supplies:

- A pad of sticky notes

You will need to set this activity up in a room with an open wall, where there is no furniture to impede your children from jumping up to grab sticky notes off the wall.

Prior to the exercise, fix a line of sticky notes from the top of the ceiling down to the eye level of your child. Curl the bottom edges of the notes, so they lift off the wall, making them easier to grab. Explain to your child that they are playing the part of the Pharisee, and you will play the part of Jesus. The object of the game is to see how many sticky notes they can grab.

If they successfully grab all the notes on the first try, they win a place in heaven. They only get one try at each note. They can ask for your help to grab any of the notes, or they can try to grab them without your help. (Don't emphasize this rule—simply state the rules. Most children will try to do this on their own until they fail and that's what you want to happen.) They only get one try.

Each time they attempt a note they should say one of two things. If they want help, they can say, "help", and you can get the note for them. If they want to grab it on their own they should say, "self-righteous", and then grab the note for themselves.

Have them start with the lowest note, which should be easily within their reach. Most kids will pride themselves in doing this exercise without help until they fail. Remember, the moment they miss a note on the very first try, you must stop them and say they failed.

If they fail, ask them why they didn't ask for help from the beginning. Their answer will likely be that they thought they could do it on their own. Use this exercise to explain how the Pharisees thought they could obey all the commandments on their own. They thought they could earn their own righteousness (goodness before God) by obeying the Law. When Jesus came, they rejected his help and refused to believe.

If your child is wise and asks for your help early, complement them on their wisdom in asking for help. Teach the same material about the Pharisees in the paragraph above and then go on to say, the tax collectors and sinners who came to Jesus knew they could not keep the Law on their own. They put their trust in Jesus to save them from their sin.

Day One

Listen Up

Read Luke 18:9–14:

> *He also told this parable to some who trusted in themselves that they were righteous, and treated others with contempt: "Two men went up into the temple to pray, one a Pharisee and the other a tax collector. The Pharisee, standing by himself, prayed thus: 'God, I thank you that I am not like other men, extortioners, unjust, adulterers, or even like this tax collector. I fast twice a week; I give tithes of all that I get.' But the tax collector, standing far off, would not even lift up his eyes to heaven, but beat his breast, saying, 'God, be merciful to me, a sinner!' I tell you, this man went down to his house justified, rather than the other. For everyone who exalts himself will be humbled, but the one who humbles himself will be exalted."*

Think about It

Our sinful nature tempts us to compare ourselves with others and look down upon their weaknesses and mistakes. Did you ever catch yourself saying things like, "I would never do that" or "I can't believe he did that" about another person's sin or mistake? While it might make us feel better, focusing on other people's failures usually means that we miss seeing our own. Soon we think we are better than others and become like the Pharisee in the parable thinking we are better than others and don't need Jesus.

The Pharisee in the parable felt good about himself because he compared his life to the tax collector. Tax collectors were dishonest and cheated the people. It is easy to feel superior (better than others) when you compare yourself to a person with greater struggles. But what if the Pharisee compared himself to the widow who deposited her last two copper coins in the temple offering? (Luke 21:1–4). Compared to her, the Pharisee wouldn't look so righteous (good).

So while the Pharisee focused on the other man's sin, he missed looking at his own heart and didn't see his need for God. Notice that his prayers were "I" focused: "I thank you that I am not like the other men." He was praying to God but praising himself. The Pharisee depended upon his own good deeds for his salvation, not the work of Jesus.

The tax collector's prayer was very different. He was certain that God was his only hope. He called out, "God, be merciful to me, a sinner!" Mercy is what motivated God to send Jesus to die upon the cross for our sin. God looked down at his children and saw us caught in sin and rebellion. God felt such tremendous compassion and love toward us that he sent his only Son to die in our place that we might be forgiven. Instead of judgment, God bestows forgiveness to those who call on him for help. The tax collector, Jesus tells us, went home justified—forgiven by God and declared innocent. The Pharisee didn't see his need for God's help. He walked away that day, still under God's judgment for thinking his good works would save him.

Talk about It

▶ What is the difference between the Pharisee and the tax collector in this parable? *(Parents, draw out your children here. The main difference is that the Pharisee is trusting in his own work for his salvation, while the tax collector is calling out to God, knowing he is a sinner. He was trusting in God to forgive him.)*

▶ Can you think of a time when you compared yourself to someone else to make yourself look better? Did you ever think you were stronger, faster, smarter, or wiser than a sibling or friend? *(Parents, share an example from your own life, then help your children think of one from their own. Often when they tattle on a sibling this comparison is at work in their heart.)*

▶ What does Jesus mean when he says, "everyone who exalts himself will be humbled, but the one who humbles himself will be exalted"? *(The Bible teaches that God opposes the proud but gives grace to the humble (James 4:6). So the proud person stands in opposition to God and will be humbled by God. But the humble person, who sees his or her sin and calls out to God for help, like the tax collector, will be forgiven. When Jesus returns to earth, all of us who placed our trust in him will reign with Jesus victorious. We will be exalted (lifted up) and changed. We will receive new glorified bodies and even given a reward for the good things we did while on earth.)*

Pray about It

Take time to confess your sin and ask God to forgive you.

Going Deeper

Jesus came to save the worst of sinners to show that God is willing to welcome anyone into his family who trusts in Jesus. While the Parable of the Pharisee and Tax Collector was only a story, Jesus did reach out to and save tax collectors in his ministry.

One day early in his ministry, Jesus walked by Matthew's tax collecting table and called him with two words, *follow me*. Matthew stood up, left his tax collecting business and became a disciple. Later, he even wrote one of the gospels. Listen as Matthew describes his encounter with Jesus, "As Jesus passed on from there, he saw a man called Matthew sitting at the tax booth, and he said to him, 'Follow me.' And he rose and followed him" (Matthew 9:9).

Zacchaeus was a chief tax collector who climbed a tree to see Jesus (Luke 19:2). Jesus walked up to him, called him down, and invited himself over to the man's house for dinner. Zacchaeus instantly turned from his sinful ways and placed his trust in Jesus.

Luke also tells us, "Now the tax collectors and sinners were all drawing near to hear him. And the Pharisees and the scribes grumbled, saying, 'This man receives sinners and eats with them'" (Luke 15:1–2). So, while the Parable of the Pharisee and Tax Collector is likely a fictitious story, it parallels what was happening in real life.

Day Two

Listen Up

Read Matthew 21:28–32:

> *"What do you think? A man had two sons. And he went to the first and said, 'Son, go and work in the vineyard today.' And he answered, 'I will not,' but afterward he changed his mind and went. And he went to the other son and said the same. And he answered, 'I go, sir,' but did not go. Which of the two did the will of his father?" They said, "The first." Jesus said to them, "Truly, I say to you, the tax collectors and the prostitutes go into the kingdom of God before you. For John came to you in the way of righteousness, and you did not believe him, but the tax collectors and the prostitutes believed him. And even when you saw it, you did not afterward change your minds and believe him.*

Think about It

Jesus taught the Parable of the Two Sons to a group of chief priests and elders who came up to him at the temple. They were trying to trap him so they would have some reason to arrest him. But just like at other times, Jesus refused to fall into their trap and told the Parable of the Two Sons.

The first son represents the most hated of all the sinners. His refusal to obey his father is a picture of the tax collectors and sinners turning away from God the Father to live a life of sin.

The second son represents the Pharisees and elders. Although he initially agreed to obey his father, he then refused. He is like the Pharisees who said they follow God and obey his Word but then refused to believe that Jesus was the Son of God, the Messiah (promised deliverer). To be certain the religious rulers understood the parable, Jesus rebuked them in saying the Tax Collectors and Prostitutes would go to heaven before the Pharisees. The Pharisees and elders looked good on the outside and did religious things like go to the temple, pray, and give large gifts, but inside their hearts, they did not trust in Jesus. In the end, the very same men turned against Jesus and planned to kill him. They were just like the rebellious son who said he would go into the vineyard (they said they obeyed God's Word) but disobeyed and did not go (they refused to trust and believe in Jesus).

Talk about It

▶ How did Jesus know the details of the Pharisees' lives and whether or not they believed in John the Baptist's message? *(While Jesus was a man, he was also God who knows all things. Jesus knew what the Pharisees were thinking even without hearing what they were saying. God knows our hearts and what we believe and trust inside.)*

▶ Which son in the parable represents the sinners and which son represents the Pharisees? *(The first son who initially disobeyed but later obeyed represents the sinners who first turned away from God but then repented. The Pharisees are represented by the second son, who said he would obey but never did. They said they followed God's Word, but when the prophecies pointed to Jesus as the deliverer of Israel, they refused to believe or follow him.)*

▶ What about us? Which son is most like us? *(We could be like either son. We are all born as sinners. Those who repent and believe in Jesus are like the first son. Others pretend to be Christians by going to church or saying they are Christians, but inside their hearts, they don't believe. They are like the second son. The question for all of us is which son are we most like? Parents, take time to share from your own life, which of the two sons you were most like before you started trusting in Jesus. Then draw out your children.)*

Pray about It

Ask God to help you turn away from your sin and trust in Jesus.

Going Deeper

Jesus told the Parable of the Two Sons to a group of Pharisees who demanded Jesus tell them who gave him the authority to teach and heal people (Matthew 21:23). Instead of answering their question, Jesus outsmarted them with a question of his own. He asked them if John's baptism was from heaven or man. The religious rulers were afraid to answer. If they said it was from heaven, then the logical question was, "So why didn't you follow John's call to repentance?"

When John the Baptist came on to the scene and challenged God's people to repent, many sinners listened and turned away from their sinful ways. John called the religious rulers a bunch of snakes (Matthew 3:7) and commanded them to turn away from their sin (Matthew 3:8). But the religious rulers, who said they followed God's Word refused to believe or turn away from their sin.

If they said it was from man and not God, they would risk the revolt of the people since they all believed John was a prophet, sent by God. So in order to protect themselves, they said they didn't know. Since they refused to answer, Jesus said he would not answer their question either. In the end, they turned against Jesus and plotted to kill him. They are the rebellious son who said he would go into the vineyard but did not go. They refused to trust and believe in Jesus.

Day Three

Listen Up

Read Matthew 21:33–41:

> *"Hear another parable. There was a master of a house who planted a vineyard and put a fence around it and dug a winepress in it and built a tower and leased it to tenants, and went into another country. When the season for fruit drew near, he sent his servants to the tenants to get his fruit. And the tenants took his servants and beat one, killed another, and stoned another. Again he sent other servants, more than the first. And they did the same to them. Finally he sent his son to them, saying, 'They will*

respect my son.' But when the tenants saw the son, they said to themselves, 'This is the heir. Come, let us kill him and have his inheritance.' And they took him and threw him out of the vineyard and killed him. When therefore the owner of the vineyard comes, what will he do to those tenants?" They said to him, "He will put those wretches to a miserable death and let out the vineyard to other tenants who will give him the fruits in their seasons."

Think about It

While many of the parables were meant to hide the truth from the self-righteous Pharisees, this parable was designed to warn them of the coming judgment of God in a way they could understand. It is certain the Pharisees knew exactly what Jesus was saying. Luke, in his retelling of this story, recorded their immediate response—"When they heard this, they said, 'Surely not!'" (Luke 20:16). Then Luke went on to say that the scribes and chief priests knew this parable was against them (Luke 20:18–19).

The master of the house in the parable represents God the Father. The servants the master sent back represent the prophets, and of course the son in the parable is Jesus. The tenants represent the nation of Israel.

You would hope that the Pharisees would be embarrassed that Jesus knew their plans and desires to get rid of him—even kill him. Still, nowhere in the story do we hear of a single Pharisee turning from their sin. They may have believed that Jesus was talking about them, but they did not believe he was God nor did they place their trust in him. As a result, they did not believe what Jesus said. They didn't believe the kingdom would be taken away.

Today there are still many Jews who believe the entire Old Testament story of Adam and Eve, Moses and the Prophets, and King David and the Psalms. Yet they still refuse to believe in Jesus. It is important for us to try to help them see that Jesus is the Son of God who came as the second Adam to crush the head of the serpent, to keep the Law and fulfill the words of the prophets. We must pray that Jews will see Jesus as the Son of God and the promised Messiah.

Talk about It

▶ Who do the people described in this parable represent? *(The master of the house is God the Father. The tenants are the religious leaders of Israel. The servants are the prophets, and the son represents Jesus.)*

▶ What does the vineyard represent? *(The vineyard represents the nation of Israel, the people of God.)*

▶ How is this parable depicting the story of Jesus? *(Like the son in the parable, Jesus was sent to earth to bring a message from God the Father. The religious rulers, who used their position for their own benefit, did not listen to the Son. They arrested him and crucified him.)*

Pray about It

Thank God for sending his Son Jesus to die on the cross for our sin and ask him to help you love him and live for him.

Going Deeper

The Parable of the Tenants is a retelling of one of Isaiah's prophecies. The Pharisees would have known this passage. Perhaps that's one reason why they understood the parable. Isaiah said, "Let me sing for my beloved my love song concerning his vineyard: My beloved had a vineyard on a very fertile hill. He dug it and cleared it of stones, and planted it with choice vines; he built a watchtower in the midst of it, and hewed out a wine vat in it; and he looked for it to yield grapes, but it yielded wild grapes" (Isaiah 5:1–2).

In the prophecy, the vineyard represents the people of God. Instead of producing good fruit for the owner, the vineyard produced bad fruit, or wild grapes. While cultivated grapes are plump, wild grapes are mostly seed with hardly any flesh.

Isaiah went on to describe how God will judge the people of Israel. In the prophecy, God destroys the vineyard. The parable Jesus taught picked up on this judgment theme, saying that the master will return and remove the tenants and judge them. The Pharisees understood Jesus was accusing them, saying that the master (God) was going to judge them (the Pharisees) for the failure of Israel. The kingdom of Israel (the vineyard) would be torn from Israel and given to new tenants (the Gentiles).

Day Four

Listen Up

Read Matthew 21:42–46:

> *Jesus said to them, "Have you never read in the Scriptures: "'The stone that the builders rejected has become the cornerstone; this was the Lord's doing, and it is marvelous in our eyes'?*
>
> *Therefore I tell you, the kingdom of God will be taken away from you and given to a people producing its fruits. And the one who falls on this stone will be broken to pieces; and when it falls on anyone, it will crush him."*
>
> *When the chief priests and the Pharisees heard his parables, they perceived that he was speaking about them. And although they were seeking to arrest him, they feared the crowds, because they held him to be a prophet.*

Think about It

After sharing the Parable of the Two Sons and the Parable of the Vineyard, the Pharisees were angry with Jesus. They couldn't believe God would take the vineyard (Israel) away from them. Then they made a terrible mistake—they planned to do to Jesus what the tenants did to the master's son.

Both Matthew and Luke tell us the religious rulers planned to arrest Jesus. Luke wrote, "The scribes and the chief priests sought to lay hands on him at that very hour, for they perceived that he had told this parable against them, but they feared the people. So they watched him and sent spies, who pretended to be sincere, that they might catch him in something he said, so as to deliver him up to the authority and jurisdiction of the governor" (Luke 20:19–20).

The chief priests were afraid to arrest Jesus in the daytime, for the people believed Jesus was a prophet, and they might rise up against them. The Roman government ruled over Israel and allowed the Pharisees and the chief priests to remain in power by their grace. But if they lost control, Rome would surely remove them.

Eventually, they hatched a plan to arrest Jesus at night, accuse him with false witnesses, and put him to death on the cross. They missed the whole point of Jesus's warning in this parable.

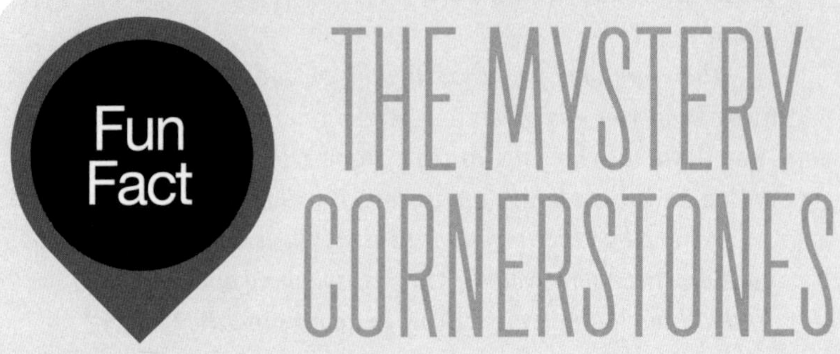

THE MYSTERY CORNERSTONES

Cornerstones have not changed in 2000 years. We use cornerstones today in the same way builders used them in Jesus day. Masons still lay their first stone in the corner to start the construction of the wall of a building. Over the years, people have come to celebrate the laying of the cornerstone to mark the beginning of construction. Often the owner of the new building will invite his friends and the local newspaper to mark the occasion.

On October 13th, 1792, the cornerstone for the White House was laid along with a brass plate marker. About one year later, on September 18, 1793, George Washington set the cornerstone in place for the United States Capitol Building on top of a silver plate. But today, no one remembers which corner block of either of these two famous buildings is the original cornerstone. (Both buildings have more than a dozen corners.) In 1991 a search was made for the Capitol Building cornerstone, but they could not find the silver plate.

As for the White House cornerstone, many presidents have attempted to locate it. Teddy Roosevelt searched, as did President Truman who sent a bomb detective into the basement to look for it but he also failed. While the location of these cornerstones is forgotten, we still have Jesus, our true Cornerstone. The Bible preserves the truth about Jesus so that anyone who looks for him will find him.

Talk about It

▶ Jesus said, "the stone that the builders rejected has become the cornerstone." Who does the stone represent, and who are the builders who rejected it? *(Jesus is the stone, and the chief priests are the builders who rejected it. A cornerstone is the first stone that's laid when building a wall of a structure. All the other stones line up with it. Jesus is the cornerstone that we are to follow. The Pharisees refused to follow Jesus and refused to listen to his teaching.)*

▶ Why didn't the Pharisees and chief priests just arrest Jesus in the daytime? *(The people believed Jesus was a prophet. He was healing their sicknesses and even raising people from the dead. If the Pharisees arrested Jesus, the people might rise up against them. This could cause problems for the religious leaders with Rome. They could lose their power.)*

▶ Who helped the religious rulers arrest Jesus at night when the crowds were back at home in bed sleeping? *(Judas, one of the twelve disciples, betrayed Jesus for a bag of thirty silver coins. One night, he led the temple guard to a place where Jesus was praying so they could arrest him away from the crowds.)*

▶ In the book of Matthew, what did Jesus say would happen to the Pharisees? *(Jesus said the kingdom would be torn from them, and those that continued to reject Jesus would not escape a sentence of hell.)*

Pray about It

Pray and ask God to help you trust and follow Jesus.

Going Deeper

While the chief priests looked religious on the outside (they wore special robes and memorized Bible verses), inside they refused to believe. Jesus called them out on their unbelief. A few chapters later in Matthew, Jesus condemns them saying:

> "Woe to you, scribes and Pharisees, hypocrites! For you are like whitewashed tombs, which outwardly appear beautiful, but within are full of dead people's bones and all uncleanness. So you also outwardly appear righteous to others, but within you are full of hypocrisy and lawlessness" (Matthew 23:27–28).

> "Fill up, then, the measure of your fathers. You serpents, you brood of vipers, how are you to escape being sentenced to hell? Therefore I send you prophets and wise men and scribes, some of whom you will kill and crucify, and some you will flog in your synagogues and persecute from town to town" (Matthew 23:32–34).

Day Five

Listen Up

Read Matthew 22:1–15:

> *And again Jesus spoke to them in parables, saying, "The kingdom of heaven may be compared to a king who gave a wedding feast for his son, and sent his servants to call those who were invited to the wedding feast, but they would not come. Again he sent other servants, saying, 'Tell those who are invited, "See, I have prepared my dinner, my oxen and my fat calves have been slaughtered, and everything is ready. Come to the wedding feast."' But they paid no attention and went off, one to his farm, another to his business, while the rest seized his servants, treated them shamefully, and killed them. The king was angry, and he sent his troops and destroyed those murderers and burned their city. Then he said to his servants, 'The wedding feast is ready, but those invited were not worthy. Go therefore*

to the main roads and invite to the wedding feast as many as you find.' And those servants went out into the roads and gathered all whom they found, both bad and good. So the wedding hall was filled with guests.

"But when the king came in to look at the guests, he saw there a man who had no wedding garment. And he said to him, 'Friend, how did you get in here without a wedding garment?' And he was speechless. Then the king said to the attendants, 'Bind him hand and foot and cast him into the outer darkness. In that place there will be weeping and gnashing of teeth.' For many are called, but few are chosen."

Then the Pharisees went and plotted how to entangle him in his words.

Think about It

The Parable of the King's Banquet is the last of three parables Jesus spoke to the religious rulers the week before his death. By this time, the chief priests and Pharisees realized Jesus was speaking against them.

The king in the parable represents God. The invitation to the wedding feast is the invitation to believe in Jesus and have your sin forgiven. Ultimately, all those who believe in Jesus will enjoy a heavenly wedding celebration (Revelation 19:7). The guests who refuse represent the religious rulers who refuse to believe in Jesus. We know that instead of believing in Jesus they planned to kill him just like those invited in the parable killed the king's servants. The second group invited to the wedding represent the Gentiles (non-Jews). Since Israel rejected Jesus, God welcomed in the Gentiles. All the way back to Abraham God said he would bless "all the nations of the earth" (Genesis 22:18).

Jesus made it very clear that believing in him is the only way to participate in the great wedding in heaven. He said, "I am the way, and the truth, and the life. No one comes to the Father except through me" (John 14:6). Jesus is the only person free of sin, who kept God's Law perfectly. Our only hope for righteousness is to accept the invitation, turn from our sin, and place our hope and trust in Jesus.

The required wedding clothes that everyone at the banquet were wearing stand for the righteousness (good works) of Jesus that God gives everyone who believes in Christ. When we come to Jesus, we exchange our sin for the perfect sinless life of Jesus. The man who came to the wedding without robes represents a person trying to get into heaven without believing in Jesus. Those who refuse to trust in Jesus do not have their sins forgiven. Their robes are still dirty with sin. There is no way God will allow sin into heaven. So the question we must ask ourselves is, what about us, are our sins forgiven? If we were to stand before God, would we be wearing bright white wedding clothes because of our belief in Jesus, or would we be like the Pharisees, wearing the stained garments of unbelief?

Talk about It

▸ How is the Parable of the King's Banquet like the other two parables (the Parable of the Two Sons and the Parable of the Vineyard)? *(Jesus taught all three parables on the same day to the same people, a group of Pharisees who refused to believe in him. All three parables are meant to warn the Pharisees against the coming judgment that will fall upon them if they refuse to believe.)*

▸ What message is Jesus trying to teach the chief priests and Pharisees in the Parable of the King's Banquet? *(The parable is teaching that there is only one way to heaven. You must accept God's invitation and trust in Jesus. No one can participate in the wedding feast apart from wearing the robes of righteousness that come from believing in Jesus.)*

▸ How did the religious rulers respond to all these warnings? *(It is clear from what Matthew and Luke tell us that they knew what Jesus was saying. Still, the religious rulers refused to believe, even after Jesus warned them. Matthew records their tragic response:* the Pharisees went and plotted how to entangle him in his words. *Instead of thinking about what Jesus said, they left seeking a way to destroy him.)*

Pray about It

Ask God to pour out his grace on you to believe. Ask God to open your eyes to see there is only one way into the wedding feast, and we all need the righteous robes of Jesus to attend.

Going Deeper

God invited the Gentiles and the outcasts—the sinners and tax collectors—to the wedding banquet of his Son. The wedding garments given represent the robes of righteousness God provides. Jesus lived a perfect life of righteousness (goodness) and offers to exchange his robes of righteousness for our sinful lives. He takes our sin upon himself and gives us his perfect righteousness in return. Isaiah prophesied about these wedding robes when he said, "I will greatly rejoice in the Lord; my soul shall exult in my God, for he has clothed me with the garments of salvation; he has covered me with the robe of righteousness, as a bridegroom decks himself like a priest with a beautiful headdress, and as a bride adorns herself with her jewels" (Isaiah 61:10).

By refusing Jesus and trusting in their ability to obey the Law, the self-righteous Pharisees and chief priests were refusing the perfect righteousness of Jesus. They are the man who appeared at the wedding without the proper wedding garments, whom the king had thrown into the outer darkness (hell) where there is weeping and gnashing of teeth.

Week 13

The Return of Christ

Let's Look at the Week. . .

Most of Matthew 21 through 23 is a record of Jesus rebuking the scribes, Pharisees, and chief priests for refusing to believe. After this lengthy rebuke of the religious rulers, Jesus prayed for Jerusalem, the city that "kills the prophets" (Matthew 23:37). Then at the start of chapter 24, Matthew recorded an alarming prediction Jesus made regarding the buildings of the temple. Jesus said to those gathered, "You see all these, do you not? Truly, I say to you, there will not be left here one stone upon another that will not be thrown down" (Matthew 24:2). Not only did Jesus criticize the Pharisees, now he was predicting the destruction of the temple. This prediction angered the Pharisees.

Later, as the disciples walked with Jesus to the Mount of Olives they pondered his comments regarding the destruction of the temple. They questioned him, "Tell us, when will these things be, and what will be the sign of your coming and of the end of the age?" (Matthew 24:3)

The disciples were seeking specific answers regarding the time of the temple's destruction and the sign of Jesus's return. Jesus's response is rather difficult to understand.

In response, Jesus provided the disciples with the signs of the coming destruction of the temple and a series of parables designed to teach them one important lesson—be ready. This week we will take a look at the answer Jesus gave.

Get Ready

The action word of the week is prepare.

The word *prepare* means to get ready. We often prepare for the weather. We listen to the weather forecast and then we prepare by picking out the right clothes. If it is going to be a really cold day, we prepare for the coming cold by wearing warm clothes. If it is going to be a rainy day, we prepare for the coming rain by taking along an umbrella.

If we fail to properly prepare for a cold, windy day by not wearing a hat, we suffer the consequence of having cold ears. If we refuse to take an umbrella when it looks like rain, we might get soaked in a storm.

The Bible tells us that we should prepare ourselves for Jesus's return. This week we will study the Parable of the Ten Virgins. Five of them came prepared for a long wait with extra oil, but the other five were not prepared, they were not ready and ran out of oil. We must ask ourselves: are we prepared for Jesus's to return? Are we ready for him to come again?

When Will the Mail Carrier Come?

(The goal of this activity is to create and experience a sense of anticipation.)

Gather your children together on a Saturday or other day when they are off of school and ask, "When do you think the mail carrier will arrive?"

Most folks receive their mail delivery around the same time each day, so your children should have a general idea what time it arrives. But for this exercise, have each person in your family guess the exact time, by the minute, of when the mail will come. To make things interesting, give each child four guesses, one in each 15-minute increment of time around when the mail normally comes. So if your mail comes at 5:00 p.m., have them guess a time between 4:30 and 4:45, 4:45 and 5:00, 5:00 and 5:15 and so forth. That way you are helping them all get close to the anticipated time, even if the mail arrives early or late. Picking extra times will add to the anticipation.

As you wait together for the mail carrier, foster a sense of anticipation and excitement among your family members. Then, compare this experience with our anticipation for the return of Christ. Jesus says we should be watchful for his return. But unlike the mail carrier, who we know comes every day around the same time, we don't know the day or hour of Jesus's return. Only God the Father knows. That's why we must always be prepared for his return by placing our trust in Jesus. When we believe in Jesus, our sins are washed away. Those who believe in Jesus and have their sins forgiven are prepared for him to come back as judge, no matter when he comes.

As believers, we should always be living with a sense of anticipation and expectation. If you needed to send a letter in the mail, but you didn't know when the mail carrier would come, you would want to be sure to get your letter into the mailbox early, so you would not miss the mail carrier. The same is true about Jesus's return. Since we don't know the hour, we should be ready now. The way we get ready for Jesus's return is to believe in Jesus and live for him today. Those who believe and trust in Jesus will rejoice the day the trumpet blows, and Jesus comes back upon the clouds. But it will be too late for those who reject Jesus—they won't be ready.

Day One

Listen Up

Read Matthew 24:15–21 and 29–35:

> *"So when you see the abomination of desolation spoken of by the prophet Daniel, standing in the holy place (let the reader understand), then let those who are in Judea flee to the mountains. Let the one who is on the housetop not go down to take what is in his house, and let the one who is in the field not turn back to take his cloak. And alas for women who are pregnant and for those who are nursing infants in those days! Pray that your flight may not be in winter or on a Sabbath. For then there will be great tribulation, such as has not been from the beginning of the world until now, no, and never will be.*
>
> *"Immediately after the tribulation of those days the sun will be darkened, and the moon will not give its light, and the stars will fall from heaven, and the powers of the heavens will be shaken. Then will appear in heaven the sign of the Son of Man, and then all the tribes of the earth will mourn, and they will see the Son of Man coming on the clouds of heaven with power and great glory. And he will send out his angels with a loud trumpet call, and they will gather his elect from the four winds, from one end of heaven to the other.*
>
> *"From the fig tree learn its lesson: as soon as its branch becomes tender and puts out its leaves, you know that summer is near. So also, when you see all these things, you know that he is near, at the very gates. Truly, I say to you, this generation will not pass away until all these things take place. Heaven and earth will pass away, but my words will not pass away.*

Think about It

When winter gives way to spring in northern climates, the buds on bare branches swell and burst open to reveal fresh green leaves. Once those leaves spread and grow, you know summer is near. Jesus told this short parable about the budding of the fig tree to emphasize the importance of understanding the signs that would signal the destruction of the temple and Jesus's return to judge the earth.

The difficulty of understanding this passage is trying to figure out which signs point to the destruction of the temple and which signs point to Jesus's return to judge the earth. In some cases, the signs point to both events.

We know that forty years after Jesus spoke these words, the Romans sacked Jerusalem and completely destroyed the temple. Today, not a single stone of the temple remains a top another, just as Jesus predicted. Jesus warned the disciples of the coming evil of those days and warned them to flee to the mountains when the signs he listed came to pass. Josephus, a Roman historian who recorded the events surrounding the destruction of Jerusalem, said so many Jews were killed that rivers of blood flowed in the streets of the city. Only those who ran from the city to the mountains were spared.

There is a broader message of warning for us in the signs Jesus gave to his disciples. Like the Pharisees who rejected Jesus, people today still refuse to believe. They don't believe Jesus is the Son of God. They don't believe or follow what Jesus said. They don't believe they will be judged for their sin, nor do they believe in a place called hell where Jesus said there will be weeping and gnashing of teeth.

But Jesus's accurate prediction, regarding the destruction of the temple—that not a single stone of the temple would be left on top another—should get our attention. If Jesus was right about the temple we should believe that he is also right about the judgment that's coming at the end of the world. When that day comes, only those who trust in Jesus will be saved. Just as Jesus's words regarding the destruction of the temple did not pass away without coming true, so will his words of final judgment come to pass.

Talk about It

▶ What did Jesus want to teach through the Parable of the Fig Tree? *(Jesus used the Parable of the Fig Tree as a word picture to teach the disciples to pay attention to the warnings he gave.)*

▶ Jesus said one day he is going to return again (Matthew 24:30). How can we be sure that Jesus is really going to come again? *(Jesus predicted that the temple would be destroyed and it happened as he said. If Jesus can predict the destruction of the temple, then he also surely knows of his return, and we can trust that his words are true.)*

▶ Why would God allow the temple to be destroyed? *(Once Jesus died for our sins, we didn't need the physical temple anymore. When Jesus was in the temple he said, "Destroy this temple, and in three days I will raise it up" [John 2:19]. But he was not referring to the temple building. He was referring to his own body. If the temple had not been destroyed, people would still be sacrificing animals today instead of trusting in Jesus.)*

Pray about It

Praise God that we don't have to sacrifice animals at the temple. All we have to do is worship Jesus. Jesus's death on the cross is the final sacrifice for our sin.

Going Deeper

In today's passage Jesus said, "when you see the abomination of desolation spoken of by the prophet Daniel, standing in the holy place (let the reader understand), then let those who are in Judea flee to the mountains (Matthew 24:15–16). So what is this "abomination of desolation" spoken of in Daniel?

Scripture defines sin as an abomination to God—"Cursed be the man who makes a carved or cast metal image, an abomination to the LORD, a thing made by the hands of a craftsman, and sets it up in secret" (Deuteronomy 27:15).

Daniel prophesied that a prince would destroy the temple and sacrifices:

"And the people of the prince who is to come shall destroy the city and the sanctuary. Its end shall come with a flood, and to the end there shall be war. Desolations are decreed. And he shall make a strong covenant with many for one week, and for half of the week he shall put an end to sacrifice and offering. And on the wing of abominations shall come one who makes desolate, until the decreed end is poured out on the desolator." (Daniel 9:26–27)

Most scholars believe Daniel's prophecy was initially fulfilled when Antiochus Epiphanes attacked Jerusalem around 167 BC. He killed the high priest, set up a pagan altar in the temple and sacrificed a pig. The temple was later recaptured, restored and beautified by Herod during Jesus's lifetime.

Jesus reinstitutes Daniel's prophecy to warn the disciples of another destruction of the temple by Rome in 70 AD, when those bearing the image of the emperor god, Caesar, would once again march on Jerusalem and destroy the temple.

Day Two

Listen Up

Read Matthew 24:36–44:

> *But concerning that day and hour no one knows, not even the angels of heaven, nor the Son, but the Father only. For as were the days of Noah, so will be the coming of the Son of Man. For as in those days before the flood they were eating and drinking, marrying and giving in marriage, until the day when Noah entered the ark, and they were unaware until the flood came and swept them all away, so will be the*

coming of the Son of Man. Then two men will be in the field; one will be taken and one left. Two women will be grinding at the mill; one will be taken and one left. Therefore, stay awake, for you do not know on what day your Lord is coming. But know this, that if the master of the house had known in what part of the night the thief was coming, he would have stayed awake and would not have let his house be broken into. Therefore you also must be ready, for the Son of Man is coming at an hour you do not expect.

Think about It

Forty days after Jesus rose from the dead he met with his disciples on the Mount of Olives where they watched him ascend into heaven. While the disciples stood there staring into the sky watching Jesus rise up into the clouds, two angels appeared to them. The angels said, "Men of Galilee, why do you stand looking into heaven? This Jesus, who was taken up from you into heaven, will come in the same way as you saw him go into heaven" (Acts 1:11). Since that day, people have been trying to figure out when Jesus will return. Everyone seems to forget that Jesus was very clear with his disciples about the timing of his return. Jesus said, "No one knows the hour." And because no one knows just when Jesus will return, we always need to be ready and prepared.

Jesus tells the Parable of the Thief in the Night to teach the disciples this very point—to always be ready. You don't know when a thief will try to break into your house. That's why people put locks on their doors and install burglar alarms—they want to always be ready if a robber comes in the night.

So what must we do to be prepared for Jesus's return? First, we must place our trust in Jesus. We must believe that Jesus's death on the cross is our only hope for forgiveness. Since we are all sinners, we need Jesus's perfect obedience and his sacrifice on the cross. Secondly, we need to repent or turn away from sin. That doesn't mean we must be perfect, but if we love and trust Jesus, we will want to follow his teaching and do our best to live for him.

So, since we don't know when he is coming, we should put our trust in Jesus and live for him now. Those who trust in Jesus and live for him are ready for him to return.

Talk about It

▶ What does the Parable of the Thief in the Night teach us? (Jesus used the Parable of the Thief in the Night to help us to understand that we always need to be ready. It would be nice if we knew when a robber was going to strike, but we never do. That's why we keep locks on our doors. In the same way, we need to always be ready for Jesus's return since we don't know when he will come.)

▶ What do we need to do to prepare for Jesus's return? (We need to turn from our sin, place our trust in Jesus, and believe in him.)

▶ What happened in the days of Noah to those people who were not prepared for the flood? (The whole world turned away from God in Noah's day. The Bible tells us their deeds were evil all the time (Genesis 6:5). Noah and his family were the only ones who believed and trusted in God. It took Noah and his sons many years to build the ark so they could be ready for God's judgment. In all that time the rest of the community around them still refused to believe. Once Noah and his family were in the ark, and the rains started to pour down, it was too late for the rest of the people. They were not ready and died in the floodwaters.)

Pray about It

Ask God to help each person in your family repent of their sin and place their hope in Jesus so everyone is ready for Jesus's return.

Going Deeper

When Jesus returns, all those who believe in him will be filled with joy as they are caught up in the air to be with him. Paul said we should encourage one another with the reminder that Jesus is coming again.

"For this we declare to you by a word from the Lord, that we who are alive, who are left until the coming of the Lord, will not precede those who have fallen asleep. For the Lord himself will descend from heaven with a cry of command, with the voice of an archangel, and with the sound of the trumpet of God. And the dead in Christ will rise first. Then we who are alive, who are left, will be caught up together with them in the clouds to meet the Lord in the air, and so we will always be with the Lord. Therefore encourage one another with these words" (1 Thessalonians 4:15–18).

But imagine how scary it will be for those who rejected Jesus and refused to believe. When the trumpet sounds at the return of Christ, they will suddenly realize that Jesus is real and his Word is true. But it will be too late for them to repent.

"Then the kings of the earth and the great ones and the generals and the rich and the powerful, and everyone, slave and free, hid themselves in the caves and among the rocks of the mountains, calling to the mountains and rocks, 'Fall on us and hide us from the face of him who is seated on the throne, and from the wrath of the Lamb, for the great day of their wrath has come, and who can stand?'" (Revelation 6:15–17)

Day Three

Listen Up

Read Matthew 25:1–13:

> *"Then the kingdom of heaven will be like ten virgins who took their lamps and went to meet the bridegroom. Five of them were foolish, and five were wise. For when the foolish took their lamps, they took no oil with them, but the wise took flasks of oil with their lamps. As the bridegroom was delayed, they all became drowsy and slept. But at midnight there was a cry, 'Here is the bridegroom! Come out to meet him.' Then all those virgins rose and trimmed their lamps. And the foolish said to the wise, 'Give us some of your*

oil, for our lamps are going out.' But the wise answered, saying, 'Since there will not be enough for us and for you, go rather to the dealers and buy for yourselves.' And while they were going to buy, the bridegroom came, and those who were ready went in with him to the marriage feast, and the door was shut. Afterward the other virgins came also, saying, 'Lord, Lord, open to us.' But he answered, 'Truly, I say to you, I do not know you.' Watch therefore, for you know neither the day nor the hour.

Think about It

The Parable of the Ten Virgins is one of three parables in a row that teach us to be ready for Jesus's return. The ten young ladies were the bridesmaids invited to join the wedding procession and feast. Five of these young ladies came prepared with extra oil and five did not. When the warning shout announced the bridegroom's arrival, five of the women were low on oil and had to leave to purchase more.

As was true in the other parables, the characters are a representation of people and concepts in our world today. Jesus is the bridegroom. He even called himself the bridegroom, saying, "Can the wedding guests mourn as long as the bridegroom is with them?" (Matthew 9:15)

The ten virgins represent all the people of the world. The five foolish bridesmaids that left to buy more oil missed the procession and were late to the feast. When they finally found more oil, it was too late, and they were not allowed in. One day when Jesus returns for his bride, it will be too late for those who refused to believe. Only those who placed their faith and trust in Jesus will be welcomed into the wedding feast of heaven.

In the Bible, oil often refers to the Holy Spirit. When we believe in Jesus, he fills us with the Holy Spirit. Those who have that oil (the Holy Spirit living with them) will be ready when the Bridegroom returns.

Talk about It

▶ Who does the bridegroom represent in the parable and who are the bridesmaids? *(Jesus is the Bridegroom, and we are the bridesmaids. Some of us are ready for the Bridegroom, and some of us are not. Revelation 21 describes the church, or people of God, as the bride of Christ.)*

▶ When might Jesus, the Bridegroom return? *(We don't know when Jesus will return. We learned that only the Father knows the date and time. By trusting in Jesus, we are prepared for his return.)*

▶ What message is this parable trying to teach us? *(Jesus is trying to teach us to be prepared for his return. Some people think they have plenty of time to live for God and believe in Jesus. We know that Jesus ascended to heaven 2000 years ago. That was a very long time ago. Surely we must be getting close to his return. We should expect the shout and the blast of the trumpet in our lifetime. That's why we need to be ready.)*

Pray about It

Ask Jesus to help you be like the wise bridesmaids who had oil. Ask him to fill you with his Holy Spirit and transform your heart so that you are ready for the return of Christ.

Going Deeper

The prophet Isaiah foretold of a day when God's people would shine with righteousness and salvation. He also compared God to a bridegroom, saying, "as the bridegroom rejoices over the bride, so shall your God rejoice over you" (Isaiah 62:5).

Later in Matthew, Jesus also described himself as the bridegroom, "And Jesus said to them, 'Can the wedding guests mourn as long as the bridegroom is with them? The days will come when the bridegroom is taken away from them, and then they will fast'" (Matthew 9:15).

The Bible refers to the people of God, the church, as the bride, "Let us rejoice and exult and give him the glory, for the marriage of the Lamb has come, and his Bride has made herself ready" (Revelation 19:7). John goes on to describe a great wedding feast at the return of Christ, "And the angel said to me, 'Write this: Blessed are those who are invited to the marriage supper of the Lamb.' And he said to me, 'These are the true words of God'" (Revelation 19:9).

Day Four

Listen Up

Read Matthew 25:14–30:

> *"For it will be like a man going on a journey, who called his servants and entrusted to them his property. To one he gave five talents, to another two, to another one, to each according to his ability. Then he went away. He who had received the five talents went at once and traded with them, and he made five talents more. So also he who had the two talents made two talents more. But he who had received the one talent went and dug in the ground and hid his master's money. Now after a long time the master of those servants came and settled accounts with them. And he who had received the five talents came forward, bringing five talents more, saying, 'Master, you delivered to me five talents; here I have made five talents more.' His master said to him, 'Well done, good and faithful servant. You have been faithful over a little; I will set you over much. Enter into the joy of your master.' And he also who had the two talents came forward, saying, 'Master, you delivered to me two talents; here I have made two talents more.' His master said to him, 'Well done, good and faithful servant. You have been faithful over a little; I will set you over much. Enter into the joy of your master.' He also who had received the one talent came forward, saying, 'Master, I knew you to be a hard man, reaping where you did not sow, and gathering where you scattered no seed, so I was afraid, and I went and hid your talent in the ground. Here you have what is yours.' But his master answered him, 'You wicked and slothful servant! You knew that I reap where I have not sown and gather where I scattered no seed? Then you ought to have invested my money with the bankers, and at my coming I should have*

received what was my own with interest. So take the talent from him and give it to him who has the ten talents. For to everyone who has will more be given, and he will have an abundance. But from the one who has not, even what he has will be taken away. And cast the worthless servant into the outer darkness. In that place there will be weeping and gnashing of teeth.'

Think about It

A talent is a measure of weight from biblical times. A talent of gold weighed 75 pounds, worth several million dollars. So even the servant who received one talent was given a large sum of money to invest. Two of the servants loved their master and faithfully put his money to work while he was gone. But the third servant acted differently. He complained. He viewed the master as a difficult man and accused him of stealing from those who planted the seeds.

Instead of faithfully investing the money entrusted to him, the third servant buried the money. When the master returned, he encouraged the first two servants for their faithfulness. But he rebuked the third servant and cast him into the outer darkness where there is "weeping and gnashing of teeth". This is a picture of those who do not trust in Jesus and are punished in hell.

Like the other parables of Matthew 25, the Parable of the Talents is meant to warn us that the Master (Jesus) is coming back, so we need to be ready.

While God doesn't provide us with money to invest, he does entrust us with a great treasure. Rather than give us talents of gold, God has given us the gospel. When Jesus returns, he will ask us to give an account of how we invested that message. True believers invest the gospel by sharing it with others to bring more people to faith in Jesus. In this way, they are like the first two servants who multiplied the riches entrusted to them.

Those who believe in Jesus are faithful to the charge of sharing the gospel message with others. Our faithfulness in sharing the message is one way we are identified as true believers in Jesus.

Talk about It

▶ How is the Parable of the Talents like the Parable of the Ten Virgins? *(Both parables show a group of people who need to be prepared for the return of an important person. The ten bridesmaids are waiting for the bridegroom while the servants are waiting for the master. They both teach we need to be ready for the return of Jesus.)*

▶ How was the attitude of the two faithful servants different from the attitude of the third servant? *(The first two servants loved their master and worked with joy. They were excited to present to the master the money they gained for him. The third servant viewed the master as a hard, dishonest man and did not love him, nor work with joy.)*

▶ What special treasure has God given us to invest? *(God has given us the gospel—the message of Jesus's life, death, resurrection, and promise of new life to anyone who believes. We invest this message by sharing it with others and inviting them to believe. Jesus told his disciples to share it to the whole world [Matthew 28:19]. Parents, discuss with your children individuals with whom your family can share the gospel.)*

Pray about It

Pray that God give you opportunities to share the gospel message with others this week.

Going Deeper

Jesus uses the phrase, "there will be weeping and gnashing of teeth" (Matthew 25:30), which is a common description of hell in Matthew's gospel. He uses it again in Matthew 13:42, 13:50, and 22:13.

When we read passages like these with our children the kneejerk reaction can be to skip over the Bible's teaching on hell and just talk about heaven. But if we don't allow adequate time for teaching on God's holiness, judgment, and the punishment of hell, the gospel solution won't seem very necessary to our kids. When we grasp that apart from Jesus's death on the cross we all deserve judgment, then the gospel is the absolute best news we could ever receive.

Consider what Jesus said to his closest followers:

"So have no fear of them, for nothing is covered that will not be revealed, or hidden that will not be known. What I tell you in the dark, say in the light, and what you hear whispered, proclaim on the housetops. And do not fear those who kill the body but cannot kill the soul. Rather fear him who can destroy both soul and body in hell" (Matthew 10:26–28).

While we don't want to create an undue fear of hell in our children, we don't want to make the opposite mistake and skip over it either. It is only through grasping how bad the bad news is that we will see the good news as the best news we will ever receive.

Day Five

Listen Up

Read Matthew 25:31–46:

> *"When the Son of Man comes in his glory, and all the angels with him, then he will sit on his glorious throne. Before him will be gathered all the nations, and he will separate people one from another as a shepherd separates the sheep from the goats. And he will place the sheep on his right, but the goats on the left. Then the King will say to those on his right, 'Come, you who are blessed by my Father, inherit the kingdom prepared for you from the foundation of the world. For I was hungry and you gave*

me food, I was thirsty and you gave me drink, I was a stranger and you welcomed me, I was naked and you clothed me, I was sick and you visited me, I was in prison and you came to me.' Then the righteous will answer him, saying, 'Lord, when did we see you hungry and feed you, or thirsty and give you drink? And when did we see you a stranger and welcome you, or naked and clothe you? And when did we see you sick or in prison and visit you?' And the King will answer them, 'Truly, I say to you, as you did it to one of the least of these my brothers, you did it to me.'

"Then he will say to those on his left, 'Depart from me, you cursed, into the eternal fire prepared for the devil and his angels. For I was hungry and you gave me no food, I was thirsty and you gave me no drink, I was a stranger and you did not welcome me, naked and you did not clothe me, sick and in prison and you did not visit me.' Then they also will answer, saying, 'Lord, when did we see you hungry or thirsty or a stranger or naked or sick or in prison, and did not minister to you?' Then he will answer them, saying, 'Truly, I say to you, as you did not do it to one of the least of these, you did not do it to me.' And these will go away into eternal punishment, but the righteous into eternal life."

Think about It

The sheep in the Parable of the Sheep and Goats represent those people who believe in Jesus, and the goats are those who reject Jesus and refuse to believe. While we wait for Jesus to return, believers and unbelievers live mixed together here on earth. There are many people who call themselves Christians, but they don't love Jesus or live for him. Their words do not match their hearts. Since Jesus knows our hearts, when he returns with his angels he will judge the people and separate the two groups. The sheep, the true believers, will go to heaven, but the goats, those who never truly believed in their heart, will be sent to hell and punished forever.

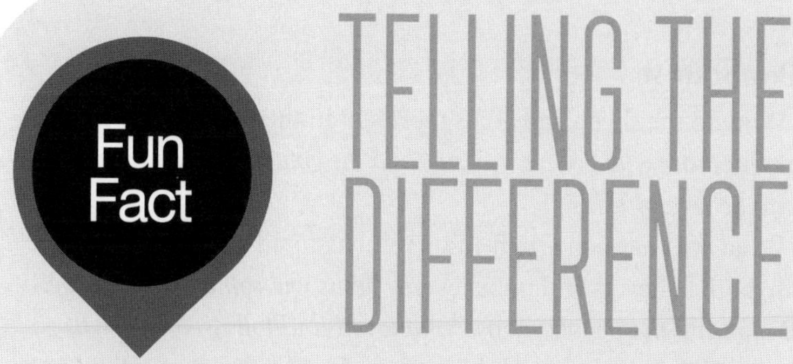

Our Bible passage today describes Jesus returning to separate the sheep from the goats. But, how can you tell the difference between a sheep and a goat? While we normally think of sheep as big puffy balls of wool and goats as skinny creatures with horns, that's not always the case. Sheep are actually quite thin after you shear their wool and sheep can also have horns. In Uganda and Kenya, the sheep and goats look quite similar. But there is one sure way to tell the difference—the tails of goats stick straight up in the air, while a sheep's tail hangs down, pointing to the ground.

When the parable mentions doing good toward others, it might seem like Jesus is teaching that those good works earn us a ticket into heaven. Jesus does say that those who gave food and drink to the needy or visited prisoners will get to heaven, but in other places in the Bible it clearly teaches you can't work your way to heaven. For example, in the book of Ephesians we read, "For by grace you have been saved through faith; and that not of yourselves, it is the gift of God; not as a result of works, so that no one may boast" (Ephesians 2:8–9 NASB).

The Bible teaches that a person can do the right thing, but for the wrong reasons. Jesus condemned the Pharisees because they did their works to look good. They didn't love Jesus; they loved themselves. Genuine good works flow out of a love for Jesus. Jesus said it like this, "If you love me, you will keep my commandments" (John 14:15). So you see, we can't become a Christian by doing good works. Rather, we do good works because we love Jesus and desire to live for him.

Talk about It

▶ Who do the sheep and goats represent in the parable? *(The sheep represent those who believe in Jesus, and the goats represent those who do not believe in Jesus.)*

▶ What will happen when Jesus returns to all the people on the earth, both believers and unbelievers? *(Jesus will come with his angels and separate the people. Those who loved and followed him will go to eternal life in heaven and those who refused to believe and did not obey Jesus will be judged and sent to eternal punishment in hell.)*

▶ Can a person get to heaven by doing good works like feeding the poor or visiting prisoners in jail? *(No, we can't earn our way to heaven. If we love Jesus, we desire to obey his commands. Jesus said that we should love our enemies and pray for those who persecute us [Matthew 5:44]. While people may try to follow this command, only those who understand the gospel—that Jesus gave up his life for us—would be willing to demonstrate that same kind of love toward their enemies. People can do good things for the wrong reasons. But only a person filled with the Holy Spirit can truly love as Jesus did.)*

Pray about It

Ask God to pour out his Spirit upon you and give you the desire to love Jesus and do good works out of that love.

Going Deeper

It can seem that there is a contradiction in Scripture between verses that say we can't get to heaven by our works and those that say we must have works to be saved. Consider these two verses:

"He saved us, not because of works done by us in righteousness, but according to his own mercy, by the washing of regeneration and renewal of the Holy Spirit" (Titus 3:5).

"What good is it, my brothers, if someone says he has faith but does not have works? Can that faith save him? If a brother or sister is poorly clothed and lacking in daily food, and one of you says to them, 'Go in peace, be warmed and filled,' without giving them the things needed for the body, what good is that? So also faith by itself, if it does not have works, is dead" (James 2:14–17).

Paul wraps these two truths together in his letter to the Ephesians. Notice how he tells us that we are not saved by works, but all those who are saved should walk in good works:

"For by grace you have been saved through faith. And this is not your own doing; it is the gift of God, not a result of works, so that no one may boast. For we are his workmanship, created in Christ Jesus for good works, which God prepared beforehand, that we should walk in them" (Ephesians 2:8–10).

While we are not saved by good works, good works always flow out of a person who is saved. Therefore, good works are an evidence of salvation. That's why we can judge a person by the fruit of their lives (Matthew 7:16).

Conclusion

The best place to end is with one of the first parables we studied together, the Parable of the Wise and Foolish Builders. Let's take a second look at the parable as interpreted in the classic hymn, "My Hope is Built on Nothing Less" written by Edward Mote in 1834. It is still widely sung today, nearly 200 years later.

My hope is built on nothing less
Than Jesus' blood and righteousness.
I dare note trust the sweetest frame,
but wholly lean on Jesus' name.
On Christ the solid rock I stand,
all other ground is sinking sand.
All other ground is sinking sand.

Now that you have read through most of the parables of Jesus, you have a choice to make. Are you going to build your house on the rock or build it upon the sand? By now you know that Jesus is the rock upon which we are all called to build. It is my prayer that through this study God has opened your ears to hear. So listen up, be a wise builder, and place your trust in Jesus Christ.